CONTENTS

PREFACE

THE BIBLE PERMEATES EVERY ASPECT of the church's life and the Christian's experience. Books have been written to compare the approaches of specific religious educators. Practical studies have centered on teaching the Bible to a particular age group. Methods of Bible study have recently become another focus of various writings. The purpose of this book is to give an overall survey of the use of the Bible in Christian education. Whatever their role teachers in churches and schools are frequently concerned about the inadequacies of teaching without realizing the many ways in which people are being exposed to the Bible. No one person has to do it all! Ministers, teachers, parents, and everyone else has a part. By reading about the many aspects of teaching the Bible, it is possible to see where one's work fits into the whole picture.

The book begins with my understanding of how the Bible is the foundation for Christian education. The next two chapters are brief introductions to two ways of understanding the Bible necessary to informed teaching. Chapter 2 outlines scholarly approaches through textual, literary, and other forms of study. Chapter 3 explores theological understandings of the Bible necessary for thoughtful study, such as the meaning of revelation, authority, and inspiration.

The several chapters that follow focus on specific practical areas. Chapter 4 is about general methods of teaching. Chapters 5, 6, and 7 discuss teaching the Bible to children, youth, and adults.

Worship, the Christian liturgy, is the primary way through which most believers come to know the Bible and its interpretation. Chapter 8 develops at length the many facets of the worship service.

Study of the Bible affects believers through two avenues: in the development of their spiritual life, which is the topic of chapter 9, and in day-to-day life, which chapter 10 discusses.

This wide range of concerns will be of help to many. Pastors may not have realized the extent to which morning worship is a learning experience. Parents and teachers may need to know more about biblical background and theological issues. Teachers as well as parents will be helped not only by the chapter on methods but by the delineation of the use of the Bible with various age groups. All readers will find useful the practical suggestions for spiritual growth through the Bible and how the discussion of the Bible helps Christians in everyday living. Professionals in the field of Christian education will have an overall survey of the subject.

Consider carefully the basic thesis: The Bible continues to be central in Christian education. We need to ask how it can also be made increasingly vital. Jesus said, "I have come that you might have life, and have it abundantly" (John 11:10). All of us who teach the Bible in any way are interpreting that life.

My particular thanks for helping in the preparation of this book go to the library staff at the School of Theology, Claremont, California, who processed endless numbers of books and cheerfully answered telephone inquiries for bibliographic information. Without a library, how could one write?

The Bible in
Christian Education

THE BIBLE IS AT THE CENTER of Christian education. No other foundation has been so widely accepted among churches, no matter how valid other approaches might seem to be to their advocates. This centrality arises from the Christian church's basis in a story— the story of God's love made known in creation and redemption through the people of Israel and through the life, death, and resurrection of Jesus Christ. This story is our story. It is the foundation and continual support of the church, the Christian community. Each member participates in that story, as it affects both the life of the individual and the interrelationships of each individual within the community. This makes the Bible the very foundation of all the church's educational work.

THE BACKGROUND

The background for Holy Scripture as the foundation of Christian education lies in the fact that many of the scriptural writings were originally intended as teaching materials. Walter Brueggemann outlines this clearly in his book *The Creative Word: Canon as Model for Biblical Education.*[1] He points out that Torah describes the ethos of God's people. The Prophets, producing tensions, hold out the possibility of new truth. The writings, including the wisdom literature, express a third way of knowledge.

---

1. (Philadelphia: Fortress Press, 1982), with specific references to pp. 12, 54, 67-68.

There are long teaching passages in the Gospels, of which Matthew 5-8 may be the best known. The teachings of Jesus are a basic component of the gospel story. The letters are filled with teaching: theological understandings as well as admonitions for living as Christians in the church and in the wider community. Other Christian writings from the early centuries continue this tradition, one of which is titled *Didache* or "Teaching."

Although only fragments of catechetical material remain from the first few centuries, the catechetical lectures delivered by Cyril, bishop of Jerusalem in the late fourth century, are extant. Candidates were prepared for Baptism during Lent, and Baptism was administered at the Easter festival. The basic teaching materials were the Ten Commandments and the Lord's Prayer—both directly biblical. To this was added the baptismal creed, whose basic statements are biblical.[2] Many churches have continued to expect those preparing for Baptism or Confirmation to learn these.

Visual images were important teaching devices during the Middle Ages, when literacy was the privilege of only a few. Clergy were more likely to be able to read and to write than rulers were.

The *Quem Queritis* strophe, in which the women at the tomb are accosted by the angel with the question, "Whom seek ye?" is the earliest form of English drama. It was performed in the chancel at the Easter celebration. Later, other episodes of the biblical drama were written with freer interpretation until the authorities deemed these better performed on the street than in the church. The cycles of biblical episodes called mystery plays were performed in sections by the various guilds as part of the Lenten observance.

Christian symbols had been teaching devices from the earliest centuries. The catacombs in Rome, some dating from the second century, tell the story in line drawings so simple as to seem like passwords: the cross, fish and loaf, Chi Rho, baptismal and resurrection drawings. Later, chancel arrangements with altar, candles, reading desk, pulpit, cross, Bible, and other symbols were constant visual reminders to participants in the liturgy. The cathedrals are the glory of medieval Christianity in Europe. Their windows and the carvings on the portals told the biblical story in vivid color and sculptured stone. In the Eastern Orthodox churches, the icon—a stylized painting on wood of holy figures—is both a teaching device and a devotional aid.

---

2. Kendig Brubaker Cully, ed., *Basic Writings in Christian Education* (Philadelphia: Westminster Press, 1960), pp. 32-40.

The Reformation brought about an emphasis on doctrine in teaching, as each part of the now-divided Western church tried to clarify its theology and ground adherents firmly in its doctrine (orthodoxy). Newly written confessions of faith did not supplant the use of the two ecumenical creeds, the Apostles' and the Nicene, but they were ways of defining positions. The Westminster Confession, reedited across the centuries, is a basic document in the Presbyterian church, the Heidelberg Confession in the German Reformed tradition, and the Augsburg Confession for Lutherans. The Thirty-nine Articles form a historic Anglican document. The Roman Catholic church defined its position in the documents from the Council of Trent. Confessions led to catechisms, which became teaching documents for the young and for converts.

The Eastern Orthodox church developed theological documents but was content with the basic creeds as its statements of belief.

Less structured Protestant groups, such as the Anabaptists and the Congregationalists, continued to stress a biblical basis for education. These groups, joined in the eighteenth century by the Methodists, became predominant in the newly emerging United States of America, more than two centuries after the Reformation. Although the Sunday school movement began in England (usually credited to Robert Raikes in 1780), it reached it fullest development in the United States during the nineteenth century as settlers spread across the country and made Sunday schools an important component of congregational structure. Biblical preaching, revivals, and Sunday school libraries became further avenues for biblical teaching.[3]

Biblical and doctrinal teaching was part of the school curriculum in seventeenth-century New England and in other colonies. Biblical stories and religious assemblies became incorporated into the early public school systems. Roman Catholics coming from Europe set up their own schools in order to transmit their religious heritage.

The final triumph of the Bible as the foundation for Protestant Christian education came with the beginning of the Uniform Lesson Series in 1882. Originally this provided themes that covered major portions of the Bible over a seven-year period. The same basic content for each lesson was taught at every age level, with teaching suggestions suitable for each age group from beginners (ages four to five) through adults. The outlines today cover a five-year period and may be topical units as well as chronological ones. Few publishers make this format

---

3. Robert W. Lynn and Elliott Wright, *Big Little Schoolhouse,* 2d ed., rev. and enlarged (Birmingham, Ala.: Religious Education Press, 1980).

the basis for curriculum at every age level, but it remains popular at the high school and adult levels. The Uniform Lesson Committee of the National Council of Churches includes nonmember, usually evangelical, denominations.

The influence of the Uniform Lessons Series cannot be overestimated. When group-graded lessons were introduced early in the 1920s, their materials also were biblical. The concern of these editors was to find biblical materials suitable for younger children or to meet the concerns of adolescents. When lessons for each specific grade appeared later, to meet the needs of churches with large Sunday schools, these also were based on biblical materials.

Biblical teaching was not confined to narrative, although telling the story and expressing its meaning in some kind of graphic work by the learner were basic teaching methods. The Bible was applied to the life situation of the learner. This emphasis in curriculum came at a time when the Herbartian method was popular in education. This was a four-step approach developed by the German educator Johann Friedrich Herbart (1776-1841).[4] The four steps were preparation, presentation, explanation, application. Some background to the story might be given, for example, the story told, the meaning explained, and its relevance to the learner's life made clear.

Roman Catholic educational materials remained oriented to the catechism until the kerygmatic catechetical movement, foreshadowed by the writings of Josef A. Jungmann and clarified at the Euchstatt Conference in 1960. Since that time religious education has emphasized the good news of the gospel, and teaching has been biblically oriented.[5]

Eastern Orthodox education, centering on the liturgy, incorporates biblical understandings from this dimension.

QUESTIONING THE BIBLICAL EMPHASIS

The early twentieth century brought an interest in child development, and the emphasis in education was on ways of teaching the child through everyday experiences. Religious education theorists began to apply these insights from general education to the specific settings of Christian education. They asked whether every biblical story could indeed be understood by children at any age. Their conclusion was

---

4. Cully pp. 265-74.
5. The American experience is described by Mary C. Boys in *Education in Faith: Maps and Visions* (San Francisco: Harper San Francisco, 1989).

that more thought needed to be given to identifying stories and teachings that were close enough to children's experience to convey the Bible's meaning for their lives. They dared suppose that there did not need to be a Bible story *every* Sunday. The key story could come from the experiences of children with some reference to biblical teaching growing out of that story.

The psychology of adolescent development in that same period had an influence on the developing field of youth work in churches. Teachers found that young people considered traditional Bible stories as something for children's Sunday school lessons. It seemed imperative to youth workers to begin with the concerns of youth and ask the question, What does the Bible have to say for us in this situation?

The recognition that adults needed broader approaches than a chronological study of the Bible was slower in coming. The Uniform Lesson Outlines became topical rather than chronological; this remains the planning principle from which they are developed today. Study topics prepared for adults focus on specific areas such as Bible, beliefs, personal religious living, and contemporary issues.

The question of the relationship between biblical teaching and life experience remains. Periodically an experience-oriented curriculum appears. Biblical material is incorporated; the emphasis, however, is not on learning the content but on reflecting on experiences and internalizing biblical phrases, teachings, or stories that could aid such reflection. Creative materials have come out of this approach, and teachers who are comfortable with the freedom it invites find it satisfying, both for them and the learners. But many people in churches do not recognize this approach as sufficiently biblical. The year's study does not end with a specific content of memorized biblical material. It seems too much like what learners find in school or in after-school groups, for these also are concerned about the ongoing experiences of learners.

The question still has to be asked as to what the Bible can say to individuals and societies today. This may be a utilitarian view, and may support an instrumental use of the Bible, yet it has always been so. The biblical writings were put together to speak to people in need and to preserve a heritage. The Bible has persisted in speaking to people through millennia and in cultures different from the ones in which it was written not only because it is called Holy Scripture but because people and communities hear the Word of God in its pages. Asking if it is relevant is a new question. Even when doctrine was dominant in Christian education, this was buttressed by scriptural references.

The persistent twentieth-century concern with understanding and meeting psychological needs and with relating to sociological situations has compelled educators to try to "fit" biblical materials into these interests. Not surprisingly, it is now noticed that biblical people were as human as twentieth-century people in their anxiety, pride, anger, love, and concerns. Some of them lived under similar circumstances: They were farmers and city dwellers as well as nomads. The people of the Bible sometimes lived in free lands and other times under foreign rule. There was good government as well as corruption. There was justice and injustice. There was suspicion of the stranger and concern for those in need.

There are differences that also need to be taken into consideration, however. The experiences of biblical people will not always parallel those of people being taught in churches today.

Not all Christian groups agree with this approach. They feel, as do the compilers of the Uniform Lesson Outlines, that any carefully chosen biblical passage, including a lectionary, can be applied in some way. Yet this ignores the fact if children find an application farfetched, they will simply not listen. Adolescents, having more choice, will absent themselves if they can make no sense of the material for their lives. Instead of an either-or approach, it may be more sensible to admit a combination of approaches through which the Bible can be taught in its own integrity and the concerns of young learners be addressed.

Some biblical materials, particularly in the historical books, portray stories of conflict and death. Efforts to tone down such writings distort them and neutralize their message. They need to be heard as the legitimate struggles of the people of Israel.

Although a strong core of people prefers the traditional approach—that is, beginning with a biblical topic and finding an application—others are uncomfortable with it. They feel this approach "domesticates" the biblical teaching, rendering it too simple by the effort to suggest parallels to the lives of today's hearers and avoiding some of the problems the Bible raises about God's requirement of obedience balanced with God's love.

In the effort to find "relevance" under specific circumstances, the power of the biblical message can be lost. Or whole sections of the Bible can be omitted because they do not fit the themes. With the exception of the Psalms and some passages in Job, for example, the section called Teachings is largely omitted from teaching materials. What is to be made of Ecclesiastes, Proverbs, and Song of Songs? When is the whole sweep of the historical books—Samuel through

Nehemiah—given serious study? How can the sixty-six chapters that constitute Isaiah be put in a form that will engage the attention of learners? One of the problems of biblically based teaching is that so much has seemed too difficult or too detailed. Clergy or laypeople who can study it deeply and teach it engagingly are hard to find. Written materials are equally scarce.

THE BIBLE AND THE RELIGIOUS IMAGINATION

Walter Brueggemann has titled his recent book *Texts under Negotiation* with the subtitle *The Bible and Postmodern Imagination*. "Postmodern" denotes the close of the Enlightenment (Cartesian) way of thinking, which affirmed the cognitive process as the most distinctive human capability and developed a canon of "objectivity." Today knowing can no longer be merely white, male, and Euro-American. Knowing, he writes, "consists not in settled certitudes but in the actual work of imagination."[6] It is contextual, local, and pluralistic.

The counterworld of the evangelical (i.e., gospel) imagination is radically different.[7] It posits everything on the gracious work of God under the contexts of memory, covenant, and hope. Biblical texts viewed from within this context yield different interpretations than when viewed from within an "objective" or cognitive framework.

Brueggemann also interprets specific texts within an evangelical infrastructure, in contrast to an "infrastructure of commodity consumerism." Such texts are subversive. In concentrating on specific stories, he proposed "a fresh honoring of the ambiguity, complexity and affront of the text without too much worry about making it palatable either to religious orthodoxy or to critical rationality."[8] The book concludes with an examination of several texts with the full realization of their dramatic quality. For example, Deuteronomy proposed the "jubilee year" each half century, in which all debts are canceled and all in bondage are freed. Imagine the impact on a modern society. Do we—can we—take Scripture that seriously? Colossians 3:5-17 speaks of stripping off the old self and clothing oneself with

---

6. Minneapolis: Fortress Press, 1993), chap. 1, "Funding Post-modern Interpretation," p. 12.
7. Ibid., chap. 2, p. 21.
8. Ibid., chap. 3, "Inside the Counter-drama," p. 59.

the new self. What a radical reordering for a church that clings to the old and is uncertain of the new even though that is promised by God. This requires an act of the religious imagination. The resistance, says Brueggemann, comes from believers "infected with modernity." They cannot rationalize such texts, so they reject them. Can we learn how to interpret the Bible from within its own context and within the contexts of memory, covenant, and hope? Can we simply hear the story? This is a daring suggestion for biblical study.

One of the most creative voices in religious education is that of Maria Harris, author of *Teaching and Religious Imagination*. "Teaching, understood as a work of the religious imagination," she explains, "is the incarnation of subject matter in such a way that it leads to the revelation of subject matter."[9] She describes a process that begins with concrete experience and continues through reflective observation, abstract conceptualization, and active experimentation. Through the grace of power (not the usual meaning of the word) comes re-creation. Harris encourages teachers to find freedom by "taking care, taking time, taking steps (as in a dance), taking form, and taking risks."[10] The goal of the teacher is to arouse the student to make choices. Through this kind of teaching and learning comes a sense of wonder and joy.

Because the Bible is the primary content of religious education, it is important that these voices, and the insights they offer, inform the teaching process. The radical challenge can bring more vitality to teaching and learning, by freeing the imagination and giving the courage to teach the Bible from a new perspective.

WHERE ARE WE NOW?

In almost all written curriculum materials, Protestant and Catholic, the Bible is the primary content taught at the elementary grade level. Some publishers design their materials for a constituency that expects this even at the preschool level. For many it is also used with adolescents. Other publishers offer options for adult courses with biblical material as one possibility along with courses on beliefs, social ethics, or personal religious living. Several independent publishers have large and faithful constituencies who find their materials dependably biblical year after year.

9. (San Francisco: Harper San Francisco, 1989), p. 60.
10. Ibid., chap. 9, p. 159 ff., "Making One's Own Model for Teaching."

Denominational planners, influenced perhaps by the current focus in biblical studies on "story theology," are orienting their materials toward an approach that urges learners to identify with people in the story. This is our story, and by becoming participants we can begin to understand what message it has for our lives. This is different from the traditional way of "application" because it is more open-ended. The emphasis will be discussed more fully in a later chapter.

One distinct trend is toward the use of lectionary-based curricula where the three biblical passages used at the Sunday service become the content for the course of study, usually with a primary emphasis on the Gospel lesson. The materials cover a three-year cycle. Because the same Scripture passage is used at every age level, from preschool through adult, it is a uniform lesson series.

This trend puzzles some religious educators who have seen the traditional Uniform Lessons Series become modified and used at fewer age levels. It seems to ignore the findings of psychology and education regarding human development at various ages. A question also arises as to whether one passage can yield meaning for learners from preschool to adults without distorting its meaning. Moreover this approach seems to be employing the traditional way of applying a biblical story to daily life without reference to the background of the material. Nevertheless, lectionary-based studies are becoming popular in church traditions that use set readings.

Some published curriculum materials, and many that are developed within congregations, place an emphasis on the life experience of the learner. Still, these are usually strongly biblical. Although some sessions, or units, may have experience-oriented titles, they frequently begin with a Bible story.

It should not be assumed that every congregation is willing even occasionally to try a new approach. Change may be unsettling to a congregation's perception of its task. Several popular Bible-based courses continue the traditional approach of telling the story and applying it to life. This insistence on making an application is susceptible to the same potential distortion inherent in the lectionary approach. Not every Bible story, or every biblical passage, can be applied in a parallel way to the life of an individual or a community today. The attempt to do so can trivialize the biblical passage. This is most likely to happen with children.

APPRECIATING A VARIETY OF APPROACHES

The Bible is the foundation for Christian education because through its pages Christians learn who God is and how God acts. Philosophical writings that speculate on the being and nature of God are important for questing minds. They are helpful to a believing community primarily when people are exploring doubt and faith.

The Bible is essential to the worship of the gathered Christian community and to the personal religious life of its members. Scripture readings, psalms, and other hymns are integral to liturgy. In addition they are subject to reflection, commentary, and application—and this makes them content for teaching.

Christianity is based on the story—our story as a Christian community—and everyone participates in this story. The whole of the biblical story has value in itself without any need to be "relevant" or "applicable" in a specific way. The process of Christian education could be enriched without distortion if we were willing to let the story speak for itself. Interpretation arises from the telling, a point made powerfully by Hans Reudi-Weber, who has worked for many years with lay Bible-study groups, in his book *Experiments with Bible Study*. When working with educated groups anyplace in the world, he says in his book, he could use print-oriented methods of reading and discussion. But when he found himself among nonliterate people, he realized that this could not be the basic method for Bible study. For generations the biblical words and traditions had been handed down (that is the root meaning of *tradition*) through story telling, various pictorial means, and liturgical enactment, including dance, song, and drama.[11]

The Bible story has value in itself: We live in it and through it. We receive our faith through its teachings and its people. The people of the Bible seem all too human, but that is why people today can identify with them. Called by God and responding to that call, they fall and rise in accordance to the degree that human weakness is overcome by the grace of God enabling them to fulfill their vocation. The Bible demonstrates how Christians are expected to live as people redeemed by Christ, who have made a confession of faith as his followers.

Applying the Bible to life is not a simple matter. Today's ruler would not want to "be like" David, although the story of David illustrates qualities of courage and trust worthy of emulation. To follow Jesus is not to "be like" him, because his was a unique vocation. Biblical situations will not always parallel contemporary ones.

Reading, discussion, and action with reference to Christian living have a place alongside telling the story for itself. But this necessary concern to understand what the Bible means for the Christian life need not be extrapolated from a story. Biblical passages alone can pose the

---

11. (Philadelphia: Westminster Press, 1981), "Reflections on the Way," pp. vii-ix.

challenge for daily living. The psalmist says, "A king is not saved by his great army; a warrior is not delivered by his great strength. The war horse is a vain hope for victory, and by its great might it cannot save" (33:16, 17 NRSV). Is this so? Can it be updated, or do modern weapons negate ancient wisdom? Such a trenchant passage gets lost in the limited efforts that have formed traditional Bible study. It has definite application to modern life, uncomfortably close to the contemporary scene.

This example suggests that the use of a few verses or a carefully selected passage may be the best way to hear how God is speaking to persons today through the words of the Bible. A simple word of comfort, "I have loved you with an everlasting love; therefore will I continue my faithfulness to you" (Jer. 31:3) in such a verse.

Becoming involved in the story is basic, so the methods of story, song, drama, and liturgy are primary ways of helping people identify with the texts. The "application" or "life experience" will come of itself through this participation when it really does fit.

For the goal of interaction between the Bible and contemporary personal and community experience may be developed in separate ways. Specific learning sessions, units, or experiences may refer to the Bible but not seek parallels with biblical experience. Teachers need a deep familiarity with the text in order to grasp how this can be done without randomly selecting verses to fit a theme, a process sometimes referred to as prooftexting.

People seem to be able to attend to more than one experience at a time. They listen to the radio while writing, they watch television while knitting, they drive the car while conversing. They go quickly from one activity to another. Notice the swift changes of image in children's television programs. This suggests that the traditional teaching goal of an integrated curriculum is not necessary. People make their own integrations. They will relate the Bible to themselves as they need to. Curriculum planning will not necessarily assist the process.

Other components in Christian education derive from life in community. People are part of a family, a church, and wider social units. These experiences may not be specifically biblically related, but they express the ways in which Christians live. We are in a line of succession from the people of the Bible, and this line includes those who have kept the faith through the succeeding two thousand years. We can not imitate them, but there should be a recognizable family resemblance.

In summary, the traditional pattern of telling a biblical story with an application to the learner's life is a construct that frequently does not fit either the meaning of the Bible or the lifestyle of the learner. The lectionary approach is a variant. The experience-oriented approach is weakened if teachers have too little knowledge and understanding of the biblical text to give depth to their teaching. Concern for the learner's experience in a nonreligious context is usually found in schools and need not be repeated in churches. The lessons learned through these usually do not last, because they lack the historical awareness that gives the sweep of the biblical story and connects it with the ongoing life of God's people. A curriculum change at specific points providing a historical overview of the biblical story might remedy this; say, at fifth grade, tenth grade, and for a specifically designed adult class (see chapter 7).

The solution, in order to do justice to both emphases, is to teach on two levels. Tell and enjoy the story. People and events interest young children. Older ones can get the feel of the chronological approach. Adolescents and adults are ready to study specific books— prophets, letters, Gospels. They can explore themes such as creation, redemption, covenant.

The experience component entails an ongoing exploration of what it means to be a Christian and to live the Christian life. We are a people called by God and led by God to live every day as those committed to Christ. People of the Bible help us to understand this vocation. Teachings in the Bible give us guidance.

This component might come into any class session where a concern had become an issue: famine in one country, violence in a community, the arrival of a new family to a congregation. An exploration of a specific area of Christian living could constitute a session or series, drawing on biblical material as needed.

The basic factor is flexibility. The Bible becomes less life-giving when the seeming necessity to remain with the topic of the day makes it impossible to deal with a fire that has burned out a family, a storm that has made thousands homeless, or the outbreak of war that threatens stability.

Remember also that people hear the Bible each week in worship. The homily or sermon is observed in the Christian year. The concerns of the Christian community are expressed in sermon, prayer, offertory, announcements, and Eucharist.

The Bible is central to Christian education. But it will be interpreted differently by each generation and within each culture. God's word is heard in many ways.

Learning about the Bible

You know the bible as one book, or perhaps two volumes, if the Old and New Testaments are bound separately. But the Bible is made up of many books, as its name suggests. *Bible* comes from a Greek word that means a "collection," or "library." Each book is distinctive.

To learn about the Bible is to learn about what makes each book distinctive as well as to see its unity in order to grasp the many perspectives represented there.

FINDING A CLEAR TEXT

The books of the Old Testament, the Hebrew Scriptures, were originally written in Hebrew. Two centuries before the Christian era, when many Jews were living in cities throughout the Greco-Roman Empire, a translation was made into Greek for their benefit. According to tradition, it was made by a committee of seventy scholars and has thus always been known (from the Greek for seventy) as the Septuagint.

The New Testament was written in Greek, the language of the gentile Christians who made up a large proportion of the early converts. Parts of it may have developed from Aramaic documents, the language used in Judea and Galilee, the native tongue of Jesus and the first disciples. When Latin became the common language of the people in Mediterranean lands, the theologian Jerome translated the Bible into that language, early in the fifth century. This was the standard translation of the Bible until vernacular translations were made at the time of the Reformation. The classical English translation is the Authorized Version of 1611, commonly referred to as the King James version because it was done by scholars convened by King James I of England. The basic Catholic translation was made during that same period by a group of scholars in exile in France and is known as the Douai-Reims Bible. The twentieth century has seen the compilation of many new translations in order to bring the Bible to people in more modern idioms.

None of the original writings of the Bible is extant. The oldest known manuscripts of the Hebrew Bible are a part of the Dead Sea Scrolls, discovered in 1947 in caves near the ruins of what had been a monastic community near the Dead Sea during the first century before Christ down to the time of the Jewish revolt against Rome in 66–70 C.E. Early New Testament fragments are extant, but the oldest Bible in manuscript—and that incomplete—is from the fourth century and was discovered at St. Catherine's Monastery in the Sinai late in the nineteenth century (Codex Sinaiticus). It is now in the British Museum.

Although examination of ancient manuscripts reveals that copiers took this work as a sacred task and were careful to be accurate, variants did creep in. You can see this as you look at the text and footnotes in any recent translation. In the New Revised Standard Version, for example, Ps. 90:1 reads, "Lord, you have been our dwelling place." The footnote states, "Another reading is *our refuge.*" In Matt. 19:20 the rich young man declares, "I have kept all these" (the Commandments). A footnote says, "Other ancient authorities add *from my youth.*" The New International Version indicates what scholars have long thought, that the narrative of the woman taken in adultery does not belong in John's Gospel. John 7:53 is printed after a parenthesis that states, "The earliest and most reliable manuscripts do not have John 7:53—8:11." The NRSV suggests places where the passage might have been added earlier, including the Gospel of Luke.

Such concern on the part of translators comparing ancient manuscripts is designed to help thoughtful readers understand the complexity of the received text.

Two contemporary translations into English have been cited. Other widely used versions are the Revised English Bible from Oxford and Cambridge University Presses in England and the New Jerusalem Bible, translated from a French version, used liturgically in many Roman Catholic parishes and read by Christians from all denominational groups. Today's English Version, published by the American Bible Society, is a simplified translation, useful as a first reader because of the immediacy this language brings to readers. It can oversimplify, however, and needs to be compared with other versions. A paraphrase such as the Living Bible also needs this comparison because in its paraphrasing of a text, the meaning can be altered.

STUDYING THE SOURCES

Students of the Bible ask the usual journalistic questions: Who wrote it, when, where, and why? There are not many clues, but some have been pursued for at least two centuries.

Determining who wrote each of the Bible's sixty-six books can be formidable. Ancient writers did not view authorship as we do today. There are enough biographical and political references in the early chapters of Isaiah to attribute that portion to him. But chapters 44–55 and 56–66 seem to be separate documents dating to the time after the exile, in the sixth century B.C.E. Jeremiah also contains biographical information, as do Amos and Hosea. The introductions to Luke and Acts suggest that these have a common author, for Acts 1:1 reads, "In the first book, O Theophilus, I wrote about all that Jesus did and taught from the beginning." Paul announces himself at the beginning of a letter. But there is no way of knowing the specific author of a Gospel.

Among ancient writers, the use of a pseudonym was acceptable, and there was no editorial office to keep track of the real names. To put Solomon's name at the head of a collection of proverbs might mean that the king, noted for wisdom, wrote them or that they were written in his name. Paul's name on a letter by someone who shared his viewpoint lent authority to the words.

How do scholars come to their conclusions? A writer has an individual style, evident, for instance, in word choice and sentence structure. By comparing the Pauline letters word for word, many scholars have become certain that Colossians, for example, was not written by Paul. A book's value to the canon depends not on the author but on the contents.

Source criticism posits Mark as the earliest Gospel, followed by Luke and Matthew, each of which has Markan material plus a source (called *Quelle* from the German for "source") followed by both but not by Mark. All three Gospels had other independent material, and it is assumed that oral traditions preceded the written Gospels. The writer of John's Gospel concludes by saying, "But there are also many other things that Jesus did; if every one of them were written down,

I suppose that the world itself could not contain the books that would be written" (21:25). This indicates that we indeed have fragmentary accounts of the life of Jesus. When was a book written? Introductions to newer translations offer information. Second Chronicles' proclamation of freedom for the exiles, for example, suggests a time after that event. Ezekiel's description of the rebuilding of the wall and temple at Jerusalem is dated by "the first year of King Cyrus" (1:1). Paul's letters can be dated with reference to his travels, and greetings to friends sometimes indicate where he was when writing a certain letter. But many books are not easy to date. Studies of the historical references in a text can help.

The *where* of a book is also problematical. The writer of the Revelation states that he was on the island of Patmos when the vision came to him (Rev. 1:9). Jeremiah wrote a letter from Jerusalem to the exiles in Babylon (Jeremiah 29). There are few clues to the places from which the Gospels were written. When Paul writes to the Philippians that "all the saints greet you, especially those of the emperor's household" (4:22), this places the letter in Rome.

There is more consensus on the reason or purpose behind particular writings. Mark opens, "The beginning of the good news of Jesus Christ, the Son of God." Each Gospel has a point of view. Paul's letters were usually addressed to a specific congregation, either because he knew them personally or anticipated visiting them. The Psalms, as compiled, are a rich liturgical hymnal and have always been used in Jewish and Christian worship.

These questions are part of historical-critical studies. This approach began in the eighteenth century as one consequence of the Age of Enlightenment, the effort to apply reason to all human endeavors. Since that time scholars have sought historical verification for biblical events and records.[1] For example, the discovery of an inscription at Tiberius naming Pontius Pilate as prefect of Judea (now in the Israel Museum in Jerusalem) attests to an approximate dating of the crucifixion. Court records of nations surrounding ancient Israel, such as Egypt and Assyria, help to document events in the books of Kings and Chronicles. A realization of the tragic plight of the exiles traveling between Jerusalem and Babylon helps the modern reader understand why the lament of Psalm 137, "By the waters of Babylon . . . we wept" ends in the terrible wish for the destruction of the captors' children.

---

1. Edgar Krentz, *The Historical-Critical Method* (Philadelphia: Fortress Press, 1985), is an excellent introduction.

Historical criticism places biblical writings in their own setting and acts as a hedge against interpreting the Bible in terms of modern culture. The historian looks at variants in biblical records, such as differences between 2 Kings and 2 Chronicles, the first having been written as court annals of the Northern Kingdom, the latter from the kingdom of Judah. Among the benefits of the historical-critical method, according to Edgar Krentz, biblical scholar, are its value as a research tool and its ability to shed new light on the history of Israel and the early church. The historical character of the Bible has thereby been clarified. By making the Bible sound strange to modern ears, the "different" quality of its environment is enunciated.[2]

Sociologists are another source for understanding the Bible. Building on the work of anthropologists, they seek a knowledge of preliterate cultures in order better to understand the oral traditions from which the biblical writings have come. By studying the cultures of the nations surrounding the ancient Israelite kingdoms, they can read the documents in the Hebrew Scriptures with new insight into the customs that influenced its stories, governance, and religion. Through the study of modern cultures, sociologists can make comparisons enabling them better to understand how biblical customs fit their time but may not be transferable.[3] Recent studies have focused on the Greco-Roman milieu of the first-century church, the characteristics of people from differing social strata who might have been converts, and the interaction of Christians with their environment.[4] For example, Paul speaks harshly to those Corinthians who gather as the church and then permit one to go hungry while another becomes drunk (1 Cor. 11:20-22). Does this indicate divisions among Christians of differing economic situations? Paul's injunction to women about covering their heads may have as much to do with social custom as with Paul's theology.

The understanding of sources has been immeasurably increased through archaeological work carried on in the Middle East during the past two centuries. The ruins of Solomon's extensive stables or of Ahab's palace enlivens the historical records. The uncovering of the village of Capernaum indicates something of the size of the place that

---

2. Ibid., pp. 63-67.
3. Robert T. Wilson, *Sociological Approaches to the Old Testament* (Philadelphia: Fortress Press, 1984), is a survey.
4. Basic volumes are John E. Stambaugh and David L. Balch, *The New Testament in Its Social Environment,* vols. 1 and 2 (Louisville: Westminster/John Knox Press, 1991).

Jesus made his headquarters. Egyptian inscriptions help unlock knowledge of the sojourn of the Hebrew tribes there from the time of Joseph until that of Moses.

A knowledge of the geography of the Holy Land also increases understanding of the Bible, as all pilgrims and travelers to that place have known. "As the mountains surround Jerusalem, so the Lord surrounds his people" (Ps. 125:2) is the song of pilgrims approaching the Holy City. The wilderness where John the Baptist lived and where Jesus went after his baptism lies along the now well traveled road between Jerusalem and Jericho. The sudden winds that rise on the Lake of Galilee can be experienced today. The land has changed little. It still offers insights into biblical stories.

LITERARY STUDIES OF THE BIBLE

Another approach to understanding the meaning of the biblical text is through literary study. In its broadest sense, this method seeks to describe the various forms of literature represented by the books of the Bible. In *Literary Criticism and the New Testament* William A. Beardslee emphasizes that form is an essential part of function and that the original function of the biblical writings was religious understanding. He goes on to delineate a number of forms, including Gospel, letters, proverbs, and apocalypse.[5]

Other literary forms could be noted. The psalms are poetry, liturgical materials, and personal prayers of petition and thanksgiving. The Song of Songs is poetry. The Prophets, centering on messages of warning, have a unique place in biblical literature. Stories illustrate the way God acts in Israel's life. Ruth and Jonah speak to a people returned from exile and determined to be rid of the foreigners who now inhabit Jerusalem. The message is that these too are God's people. Esther celebrates deliverance from oppression.

The literary forms of the Bible are examined in Robert Alter's book *The Art of Biblical Narrative.* As a literary scholar who has fully studied the Hebrew Bible, he understands that story can be a way of conveying truth. He writes, "Fiction is a mode of knowledge not only because it is a certain way of imagining characters and events . . . but also because it possesses a certain repertoire of techniques for telling a story. . . . [The writer can] penetrate the emotions of his characters, imitate or summarize their inner speech, analyze their motives, move

---

5. (Philadelphia: Fortress Press, 1970), p. 11.

from the narrative present to the near or distant past and back again, and by all these means [to] control what we learn and what we are left to ponder about the characters and the meaning of the story."[6] We see an illustration of the power of narrative when it does more than merely list facts in Art Spiegelman's first book, *Maus: A Survivor's Tale.* Illustrated with cartoon animals, this tells the story of his parents' tragic experience of the Holocaust. He writes, "It's fiction, in that it is shaped reality, and reality is much more difficult to grab hold of. But I really tried to stay with events that happened in real time and real space."[7] "Shaped reality": The Holocaust was real; his parents' suffering was real, but this becomes especially vivid—painful and compelling—to the next generation when what is written goes beyond the bare facts.

Much of the vividness of biblical narrative partakes of this quality. David's encounter with Nathan is not a verbatim report, yet the prophet's accusation, "You are the man," has had convicting power for three thousand years. Many people would accept the possibility that the Gospels, written a generation after the events they record, embody oral and written traditions enhanced by direct conversation and description. The object of the biblical writers, as has already been noted, was to convey religious understanding—truth. Their means was frequently through narrative.

Delineating these and other forms, Edgar V. McKnight, writing in his introductory study *What Is Form Criticism?* begins with the work of the German scholar Hermann Gunkel.[8] He demonstrated that the first five books of the Hebrew Bible, collectively referred to as the Pentateuch, were compiled from several ancient records. One, known as the J document, standing for *Jahwist,* from the name used for God (JHWH or YHWH), was probably written in the tenth century B.C.E., in Judah, during the reign of Solomon as a charter of national faith. The second, called the E document, for *Eloist,* another name used for God (Elohim), was written in the Northern Kingdom, Israel, probably early in the eighth century. These found their way to Babylon, land of exile for the southerners, and were collected by priests who added their own narrative interpretations before completing the whole document sometime after the return to Jerusalem in the mid-fifth century. An understanding of the composite nature of Genesis, for instance,

---

6. (New York: Basic Books, 1981), pp. 156-57.
7. From an interview in the *Los Angeles Times* by Russell Miller, November 22, 1991.
8. (Philadelphia: Fortress Press, 1969), pp. 10-11.

helps to explain why that book has two versions of the creation story (1:1—2:4 and 2:4-25).

Each Gospel contains certain forms. These were first outlined by the Germans scholars Marin Dibelius (*From Tradition to Gospel,* 1919) and Rudolf Bultmann (*History of the Synoptic Tradition,* 1921). They affirmed that these narratives arise out of the life situation of the early church, and materials were chosen to meet the needs of the congregations. Of the several forms in the Gospels, the most prominent is the passion narrative, constituting at least one third of each Gospel. Other materials include anecdotes, many of which have pithy endings. When Jesus was criticized while dining at the home of Levi the tax gatherer, the narrative concludes: "Those who are well have no need of a physician, but those who are sick; I have come to call not the righteous but the sinners" (Mark 2:17). There are also proverbs, apocalyptic sayings, rules for living, and legends. It helps to understand that one word used in the Gospels for miracle, *semeion,* means "sign." These acts are signs that God's power has broken into the world in a new way in Jesus Christ. The word does not bear the popular notion of an act that is contrary to natural causation.

Clearly there are many strands of materials within each of the Gospels. The purpose of form criticism, writes McKnight, is to get beyond the sources to the oral tradition and to see how the concerns of the church modified the earlier collections of the sayings of Jesus.[9]

As Gunkel suggested, referring to legendary material in Genesis, the flood story may reflect an ancient flood, but it also serves a theological purpose of identifying God's promise. The tower of Babel may refer to an ancient temple, but it also answers the question, Why are there so many languages? Truth is embodied in legend.

Rudolf Bultmann's theological writings emphasize the Christ of faith—the "Christ event" as more important for the believer than the Jesus of history. The *Kerygma,* the preaching about Jesus, was what brought people to faith in apostolic times.

Parables as a form have received considerable attention lately. In his book *In Parables* John Dominic Crossan sees the parable as a metaphor in which the listener participates. It is not a story we listen to and then apply to our lives. Referring to Matt. 13:34, which says, "Jesus told the crowds all these things in parables; without a parable he told them nothing," Crossan writes, "Parables are only to be understood from inside their own world. They are revelatory of the world only to insiders, not to any definite predetermined in-group

---

9. Ibid., p. vi.

but to the group formed in them, those who have learned to live *in parables.*" The writer goes further and raises "the deliberate question of whether there is any other way to live, and any other way to know reality, than *in parables.* It evokes the possibility that 'in reality' means no more and no less than 'in parables,' that reality is parabolic."[10] Crossan is saying that metaphor involves the person hearing it. When we listen to the parable of the prodigal, it is not a matter of standing on the outside, watching each of the players. Rather it is a matter of being each of the players.

A parable always includes a surprise element that catches the hearer off guard. In the parable of the prodigal, for instance, those who try hard to keep all the rules feel as aggrieved as the elder brother that the father should do anything so unfair as to celebrate the return of the wastrel son. Similarly no practical businessperson would consider paying the same wage to the late-coming workers as to those who had worked hard all day. Jesus confronts his hearers with the uncomfortable thought that God might not play by our rules and that God's grace is beyond human grasp. Herein lies the power of the parables as the primary form of Jesus' teaching.[11]

An intensive study of the words of the text is done by structuralists. This endeavor cannot be subsumed under textual studies, because it seeks to go beyond the received text. With antecedents in French literary criticism and the work of Roland Barthes, it is linguistically oriented. Daniel Patte, one of the foremost expositors of the approach, explains that "the structural exegete attempts to uncover, for instance, the linguistic, narrative, or mythical structures of the text under consideration. Whether or not these structures were intended by the author is not a relevant question. In fact, in most instances it appears quite likely that the author was not aware of using such complex structures. Indeed he was preoccupied with conveying a meaning." He continued, "The structural analyst studies this language without concern for what the author meant (the traditionally understood semantic dimension of the text)."[12] Structuralists are concerned to find underlying meanings in the language itself. This involves an understanding of the culture and therefore includes anthropological studies. It is countered currently by deconstruction, which seeks to uncover the ignored, problematic,

---

10. *In Parables: The Challenge of the Historical Jesus* (New York: Harper & Row, 1973), p. xiv.
11. Another excellent study of parables is Sally McFague, *Metaphorical Theology: Models of God in Religious Language* (Philadelphia: Fortress Press, 1982).
12. *What Is Structural Exegesis?* (Philadelphia: Fortress Press, 1976), pp. 14-15.

and contradictory aspects of the text. Structuralist and post-structuralists studies are still in the province of the academic world and have not yielded many practical insights for general biblical studies.

One recent method in biblical study considers texts in the light of the formal categories of rhetoric in the ancient world.[13] Scholars begin with the assumption that both Paul and the Gospel writers used these rhetorical conventions in their attempts to persuade their readers. Rhetorical criticism is also employed in analyzing Old Testament documents. It takes account of both the social situation out of which a writing arose and the author's intention in the writing. Inquiry focuses on units of material rather than on whole books. More subtle aspects refer to the authority of the speaker, something that can be noted in the writings of Paul. Applying the formal rules of rhetoric to first-century Christian writing, Burton Mack finds a number of examples of this form in the Gospels, including Mark 8:34—9:1, where the rhetorical categories include the thesis, reason, argument, analogy, example, and pronouncement.[14]

He also examines passages from Hebrews, Paul's letters, and Peter's sermon in Acts. The value of this approach, asserts Mack, is that it "explores the human issues at stake in early Christian social formation and its discourse. It seeks to render some account of the social issues that lay behind the rhetorical issues that surface in the literature of discourse. And it hopes to find some way to assess the quality of life reflected in the rhetoric, a quality that will be measured by the nature of that rhetoric itself."[15]

OTHER INTERPRETIVE VOICES

The relatively recent contributions of women scholars have had an important impact on contemporary biblical studies.

---

13. An introductory study is offered by Burton L. Mack, *Rhetoric and the New Testament* (Minneapolis: Fortress Press, 1990). In the introduction he dates the interest in this area to the presidential address of James Muilenburg at the Society of Biblical Literature in 1968, titled "After Form Criticism, What?" p. 12. Phyllis Trible's *Rhetorical Criticism: Context, Method and the Book of Jonah,* Minneapolis, Augsburg Fortress Press, 1994, has an excellent introduction to rhetorical criticism and its relationship to structuralism, deconstruction and reader response criticism, followed by an exegesis of the Book of Jonah.
14. Ibid., p. 81.
15. Ibid., p. 94.

THE FIRST CHALLENGE to male-dominated biblical interpretation came with *The Woman's Bible* published in 1895. Elizabeth Cady Stanton, irked by the exclusion of women among the scholars preparing a revision of the Authorized Version, gathered a group of women to make their own biblical commentary from a feminist perspective, although much of the work was from her pen.[16]

Inevitably the resurgent women's movement that began in the 1960s would bring women into prominence as biblical scholars. Their early efforts were designed to tear down the superstructures, challenging the patriarchy and misogyny apparent in the Bible. Feminist writers questioned the overwhelming depiction of God through male metaphors and male types of activity ("The Lord strong and mighty; the Lord mighty in battle"). They pointed out the cruel and demeaning treatment of many women in the Bible. These writers demonstrated that the place of women in church and society for two thousand years had been predicated on biblical models of subservience to men.

Current feminist biblical scholarship, by contrast, is marked by efforts to rebuild. In her book *God and the Rhetoric of Sexuality,* Phyllis Trible examines Gen. 1:27 and the surrounding text by way of affirming the common created humanity of male and female.[17] In many texts she sees clues for feminine metaphors for God. Thus in Isa. 66:13 we read, "As a mother comforts her child, so will I comfort you: you shall be comforted in Jerusalem." She poignantly describes the mistreatment of women in *Texts of Terror,* where she retells the stories of Hager, Tamar, the Unnamed Woman (the Levite's concubine in Judges 19) and Jephthah's daughter.[18]

Trible draws parallels between these ancient women and women in similar situations in New York City, where she lives.

The rebuilding has continued in the work of Elisabeth Schüssler Fiorenza. Her book *In Memory of Her,* subtitled *A Feminist Theological Reconstruction of Christian Origins,* enunciates the prominent role of women both during the ministry of Jesus and in the first generation of the church. It then describes the process across several centuries during which they were removed from leadership.[19]

Rosemary Radford Ruether asks the question, Can a male savior save women? and answers that Jesus reversed the social hierarchy and made all persons equal before God and in relation to each other ("The

---

16. The original feminist attack on the Bible (N.Y.: European Pub. Co.), pp. 150, 17.
17. (Philadelphia: Fortress Press, 1978).
18. Subtitled *Feminist Readings in Biblical Narrative,* (Philadelphia: Fortress Press, 1984).
19. (New York: Crossroad, 1983).

last shall be first"). Jesus, the marginalized one, invited the marginalized into the realm of God.[20]

Text is basic to interpretation. The RSV committee that had produced a seemingly accurate revision of the Bible in 1946 found it necessary in the 1970s and 1980s to go back to the sources and produce a new RSV, with Phyllis Trible now a member of that august group. It was discovered belatedly that there are in Hebrew and Greek two words that had been translated by one English word: one word for man/male and one for human being. The New Revised Standard Version distinguishes between the two. Revised versions of the New English Bible and the Jerusalem Bible also reflect this correction.

The question of gender pronouns for God in translation remains problematical. Christians and Jews know that God has no gender, being transcendent and immanent and not having human form. But the writers of the Bible used the male pronoun, and the Hebrew and Greek pronouns have been translated literally into English. The question of pronouns in hymns and other liturgical materials is another matter (see chapter 8).

An African American hermeneutic of the Bible uncovers the place of Africans in the biblical text. King Asa of Judah was engaged in battle with the Ethiopians. The Queen of Sheba came with her retinue to visit King Solomon. Jeremiah is saved from the pit by an Ethiopian in the king's court. The beautiful young woman in Song of Songs is described lyrically as "I am black and beautiful, O daughters of Jerusalem" (2:5). The cross of Jesus was carried by a man from Cyrene, whose sons are mentioned in the narrative as though known to the readers of Mark's Gospel. Philip the deacon baptized the treasurer of the queen of Ethiopia.

Powerful biblical interpretation is conveyed through the words and music of the Spirituals. The Exodus theme has been pervasive: the drive toward freedom as God's intention for an oppressed people. Biblical texts became subversive as expressed in story, song, and preaching. They took on personal and community meanings to become the language of hope in a seemingly hopeless situation. As God was present in the political struggles for freedom in the story of Israel, so God would be present in the political struggles for freedom among these people. Hope in the God made known in the pages of Scripture assured strength to endure the present and look toward a time of freedom and full participation in the life of community and nation.

---

20. *Sexism and God-Talk: Toward a Feminist Theology* (Boston: Beacon Press, 1983), chap. 5, "Christology: Can a Male Savior Save Women?"

The acclaimed speeches of Martin Luther King Jr. are filled with scriptural quotations or allusions. The foundation for his style is biblical.

When interpreters from social sectors long excluded from traditional scholarship bring their concerns to biblical inquiry, different perspectives come into view and the whole area of study must incorporate different perceptions.

Reader response criticism is another form of study that has become prevalent in recent years. This approach brings the response of the reader into the understanding of the text and allows the reader to generate new meanings within the potential of the text. In *Post-modern Use of the Bible: The Emergence of Reader-Oriented Criticism,* Edgar V. McKnight writes, "The reader-oriented approach acknowledges that the contemporary reader's 'intending' of the text is not the same as that of the ancient author and/or of the ancient readers." Nevertheless, he affirms, in different epochs with different world views, the Bible has spoken to different readers. . . . Dogmatic, historical, and existential approaches have all provided readers with the 'information' they needed and were prepared to receive."[21] He sees continuity in this process.

PUTTING IT ALL TOGETHER

Tradition history is considered a link between literary criticism and the broader aspects of tradition. These scholars examine the materials in terms of the groups who collected them, such as court chroniclers or priests, and the places in which they were collected—Schechem and Jerusalem, for example. They examine the social and political factors that led to the preservation and compilation of materials, such as the fall of Jerusalem or the return from Babylonian exile. They inquire about the relation of tradition to history. Involved in this is the relationship of oral tradition to written records.[22]

If this description of the many forms of literary studies of the Bible leaves the impression that the Scriptures are simply a collection of varied materials, nothing could be further from the truth. Each book of the Bible is a whole. This is emphasized by the work of those in

---

21. (Nashville: Abingdon Press, 1988), p. 150, 17.
22. For introductory study, see Walter E. Rast, *Tradition History and the Old Testament* (Philadelphia: Fortress Press, 1972). A basic study in the field is *Old Testament Theology* by German scholar Gerhard von Rad (New York: Harper & Row, 1962).

redaction criticism. The redactor is an editor, and thus redaction criticism looks at the editorial policy that governed the final form of those books that were not clearly the work of one writer. Biblical scholar Norman Perrin defines this discipline as "concerned with studying the theological motivation of an author as this is revealed in the collection, arrangement, editing, and modification of traditional material, and in the composition of new material or the creation of new forms within the traditions of early Christianity."[23] This method applies to the Old Testament (to the study of Genesis or Isaiah, for example) as well as to the New. Perrin offers the alternative phrase of "composition criticism."[24]

Today, because we expect a writer to use footnotes to indicate material from outside sources, we have difficulty understanding the editorial methods used in the writing of the Bible. When an unidentified editor carefully chose materials from the recorded chronicles of the Northern Kingdom and those of the Southern Kingdom and then added materials from the priestly context of the postexilic period, a structured literary work was the result. The theme in Genesis was the beginnings of the covenant people from creation through several generations of the tribe of Abraham and up to the entrance into Egypt. The purpose was to show how God the Creator had formed this people and was leading them in a covenant first established in the land of Canaan. The next three books move the story forward, and the fifth, Deuteronomy, recapitulates the journey. The theological purpose is the same: to proclaim God's guidance of a chosen people.

Similarly, each Gospel was put together by a different writer, and each shows a different style with some different choices of material. Mark (sixteen chapters) is the briefest of the recitals. Matthew includes more teaching materials. Luke includes more parables. John has a completely different outline, one that is not chronological. His theological basis is the incarnation: "The Word became flesh and lived among us" (1:14). John includes a series of exhortations around key words: "I am the way, the truth, and the life" (14:6), "I am the bread of life" (6:35). The book of Acts begins with Jesus at his ascension charging the disciples to be his witnesses "in Jerusalem, in all Judea and Samaria, and to the ends of the earth" (1:18). This is the geographical pattern the book follows, from Jerusalem to Rome.

That many biblical books had editors rather than authors should compel our respect for the seriousness with which they fulfilled their

---

23. *What Is Redaction Criticism?* (Philadelphia: Fortress Press, 1969), p. 1.
24. Ibid., p. 78.

task. Remember also that these books reflect the life of the communities for which they were written. The materials selected for the Gospels, for example, answer questions arising in young churches seeking to know how the life and teachings of the Lord could help them in their situation. As Perrin concludes, "Gospel material represents a flowing together of past, present, and future. It takes the form of stories and sayings from the past because the Jesus who speaks is the Jesus who spoke and because the Jesus to come as Lord/Son of Man is the Jesus who came as eschatological prophet. . . . There would have been no Gospel of Mark without the conviction that the risen Lord had a message for the church for which Mark wrote."[25]

Redaction criticism leads into the study of narrative theology. This is the assertion that the Bible is basically narrative—story—and the theology is implicit in the stories. There are blocks of laws, teachings, proverbs, and other didactic materials, but the basic thrust of the Bible is narrative.

Mark Allen Powell, in his concise book *What Is Narrative Criticism?* outlines the elements of story and describes how these are found in the biblical books. They have a point of view; they develop events, characters, and settings. He notes the use of symbols and irony. In conclusion he points to some of the benefits of this approach in its focus on the biblical narrative itself, its appeal to the nonscholarly reader, and its close relationship to the believing community.[26]

Story can be a sophisticated concept. Psychological understandings of story have given new interpretations to fairy tales.[27] Psychobiography, as a field of research, looks at the ways a people knows its history through its stories. Stories both reflect and reinforce social tradition. Thus Stephen Crites writes, "The sacred story does not transpire within a conscious world. It forms the very consciousness that projects a total world horizon, and therefore informs the intentions by which actions are projected into the world."[28]

The Gospel stories are testimonies to Jesus through his life, death, and resurrection. They are not simply memories but are memory made present (*anamnesis*). The theological understanding of Jesus Christ is

---

25. (Minneapolis: Fortress Press, 1991), pp. 85-87.
26. (Minneapolis: Fortress Press, 1990), pp. 101f.
27. Cf. Bruno Bettelheim, *The Uses of Enchantment: The Meaning and Importance of Fairy Tales* (New York: Vintage Books, 1989).
28. "The Narrative Quality of Experience," p. 71, in *Why Narrative? Readings in Narrative Theology*, ed. Stanley Hauerwas and L. Gregory Jones (Grand Rapids, Mich.: Wm. B. Eerdmans, 1989). Article originally published in *Journal of the American Academy of Religion* 39, 3 (September 1971): 291-311.

made known through these stories. They are the vehicle through which faith is awakened. German theologian Johannes Metz has a powerful suggestion:

> There can, of course, be no *a priori* proof of the critical and liberating effect of such stories, which have to be encountered, listened to, and told again. But surely there are, in our post-narrative age, storytellers who can demonstrate what "stories" might be today—not just artificial private constructions, but narratives with a stimulating effect and aiming at social criticism, "dangerous" stories in other words. Can we perhaps retell the Jesus stories nowadays in this way?[29]

The stories, the edited books, all combine in the collection of books that we call the Holy Bible. The completed collection is itself no accident. Canonical criticism is the area of study that explores how we came to have this particular selection of writings. The Dead Sea Scrolls contain all of the books of the Hebrew Scriptures except the book of Esther. Yet that book appeared later in a completed collection gathered together possibly by a group of priests from Jerusalem after the destruction of the Temple in 70 C.E. At a place called Jamnia in about 100 C.E., it is widely believed among scholars, the thirty-nine were affirmed as Scripture for liturgical use and study. *Canon* comes from a Greek and later Latin word meaning first "rod" and then "measuring rod." Certain standards of consistency governed the choice of books to be included. This is what constitutes the "unity of the Bible."

Letters of Paul and probably collections of the deeds and sayings of Jesus, as well as the passion narrative, circulated among the early churches. The limits of the New Testament canon were not set until the mid-fourth century.

In his book *From Sacred Story to Sacred Text,* James M. Sanders suggests that the binding theme in our canon is God, Creator and Redeemer.[30] Canon, he says, lends both stability and adaptability to the Scriptures. He writes, "The work of biblical hermeneutic today is to seek a midpoint between the historical-critical method, which

---

29. "A Short Apology of Narrative," ibid., p. 256. Originally published in *Concilium* 85 (1973): 84-96.
30. (Philadelphia: Fortress Press, 1987), p. 65. Another scholar writing in this field is Brevard S. Childs, *Old Testament Theology in Canonical Context* (Philadelphia: Fortress Press, 1986).

seeks original biblical meanings, and the hermeneutical task of spanning the gap between those recovered meanings and modern cultural systems of meaning." This he calls canonical hermeneutics. The principles and rules of canonical hermeneutics, he writes, are to discern the contemporary context, be within the covenant community, and recite the Torah memory.[31]

Canonical criticism then, like other forms of scholarly biblical study, begins within the believing community. As the story is recited and studied, it becomes interpreted within the context of the lives of the believers.

Distinguished literary and biblical critic Amos Wilder has summed it up:

> A Christian can confess his faith wherever he is, and without his Bible, just by telling a story or a series of stories. It is through the Christian story that God speaks, and all heaven and earth come into it. God is an active and purposeful God and his action with and for men has a beginning, a middle and an end like any good story. The life of a Christian is not like a dream shot through with visions and illuminations, but a pilgrimage, a race, in short, a history. The new Christian speech inevitably took the form of a story. The believers wanted to tell the world the way of the world as they saw it.[32]

IMPLICATIONS FOR RELIGIOUS EDUCATION

The wealth of resources available indicates that teachers should not presume that simply looking at a text will reveal its full meaning.

Teachers need to avail themselves of enrichment materials to help them understand the environment from which the biblical books came. Archaeology confirms stories; geography illumines references. Knowledge about the historical and social settings of the Bible brings its own insights.

Teachers need to make the most of the fact that the Bible consists of many literary forms. It is this variety that gives liveliness to the Bible and enlivens teaching. Curriculum materials as written and taught too often evince a sense of sameness. This ignores the clear

---

31. Ibid., p. 69.
32. *The Language of the Gospel: Early Christian Rhetoric* (New York: Harper & Row, 1965), p. 24.

diversity apparent from even a simple reading of the texts. The Bible is a living word in many senses. One of these is in the kinds of literature, the diverse characters, and the main settings.

Teachers need to study seriously the deeper meanings of the word *story*. This is the most ancient and the most powerful form of teaching and learning. Story enables the learner to participate in the lives and situations of those people to whom God was speaking and through whom God was acting. Through such participation they hear themselves addressed. Much as we might wish to believe otherwise, human nature has not changed. We are Adam, Rebecca, Mary, Peter. When the Bible is taught as story, we get beyond the oversimplification implied by the word *application*. We do not stand outside judging or scrutinize with detachment. We are part of the story.

By studying the way the Bible is written, teachers can come to appreciate the unity of Scripture within its diversity. Neither facet should be slighted. This necessitates reading the entire Bible in order to be able to position whatever segment is being taught within the framework of the whole. The fragmentation of the Bible in present teaching is a serious deficiency that makes our efforts at biblical education inadequate.

Teachers can become more aware of how the reader's personal viewpoint affects his or her interpretation. This is both inevitable and good. By sharing their personal responses, those who study together make new insights available. Teachers become learners in the process.

Literary study is part of any school curriculum, particularly for older children, adolescents, and adults. Recognizing the various forms of literature used in schools can help teachers in the church link biblical study with other learnings. For this reason, they need to incorporate into their own study and teaching of the Bible the more technical aspects of literary biblical studies discussed earlier in this chapter. Their learners need this framework in order to understand parts of the Bible that, in the traditional rational or scientific orientation of education, they might be inclined to dismiss as "fairy tales" (the children's word) or "unreal" (the adolescents' word). This misunderstanding would have the unfortunate consequence of preventing them from hearing what the biblical narrative is saying. Without the appropriate study tools, they will not hear themselves addressed by God. They will avoid the substance by focusing on the style.

These critical tools need to be incorporated in both written curriculum materials and in the translation of these materials in the actual teaching situation. Taking seriously the many routes by which the Bible has come to us in its present form is an important key to effective teaching.

Interpreting
the Bible

THE BIBLE IS ALWAYS BEING INTERPRETED. The reader inevitably
translates what is read to a personal context. For this reason, it is
important to explore some presuppositions that people bring to their
interpretation of the Bible. In none of these areas is there complete
agreement among all Christians as to the boundaries of meaning.

REVELATION

The Bible is frequently referred to as the Word of God. This may
mean the word through which God makes God's will known or the
actions that demonstrate God's activity. It could mean, literally, the
words that God speaks. The word of God in Scripture has been referred
to as that which points to the Word made flesh, Jesus Christ.

Revelation in its root means to make known that which is hidden.
It can further mean a sudden demonstration, as in an apocalypse or a
theophany—a direct apprehension of God. Revelation, then, can be
God's self-disclosure. The German theologian Wolfhart Pannenberg
affirms that in a technical sense the Bible has no term for God's self-
revelation, but speaks rather of "manifestations." God reveals someone
or something.[1] He writes, "Only after their occurrence [i.e., events]
is God's deity perceived. Thus placing revelation at the close of history
is grounded in the indirectness of revelation."[2]

---

1. Wolfhart Pannenberg, ed. *Revelation as History* (New York: Macmillan Co.,
1968), p. 9.
2. Ibid., p. 131.

Christians have interpreted revelation in a number of ways. Most will affirm that there are two forms of revelation: natural or general revelation and special (supernatural) revelation.[3] The manifestation of God in the natural world moves people to look upon the wonders of earth in land, sea, or mountain with a sense of awe and to affirm that these demonstrate the work of a Creator. People in every form of religion seem to have this awareness of the wonders of earth.

Special revelation is the disclosure that God makes to a particular people in a particular way. The action of God in the history of Israel as recorded in Scripture is special revelation. Supremely for Christians special revelation is seen in the life, death, and resurrection of Jesus Christ.

The words *revelation* and *reveal* do not occur frequently in the Bible. In Deut. 29:29 a distinction is made: "The secret things belong to the Lord our God, but the revealed things belong to us and to our children forever, to observe all the words of this law." In 1 Sam. 3:21: "The Lord revealed himself to Samuel at Shiloh by the word of the Lord." In Isa. 56:1 it is written, "Then my salvation will come, and my deliverance be revealed." In the New Testament the Father is revealed by the Son (Matt. 11:27). Paul, referring to his conversion experience, writes, "God . . . was pleased to reveal his Son to me" (Gal. 1:16). In the letter to the Romans he writes, "The righteousness of God is revealed through faith for faith" (1:17). In 1 Cor. 2:10 Paul states that the wisdom of God is revealed to us through the Spirit.

These few quotations indicate several areas of revelation. The word of God, God's glory, salvation, and deliverance are revealed. In the New Testament Christ is the revealer of God, and God is revealed to Paul through Christ.

Avery Dulles has outlined five models of revelation in his book by that name. The first model is revelation as doctrine.[4] This has characterized Protestant evangelicalism and Catholic neo-scholasticism. The Word of God reveals who God is, and this is the basis for the doctrine of God derived from the Bible. Scripture also gives the commands of God: For the Jews in Torah and for Christians in the Sermon on the Mount and other teachings of Jesus. God has revealed how God's people are to live in obedience. The blueprint, so to speak, for the Christian life is given in the pages of the Bible.

---

3. Karl Barth insisted on the primacy of special revelation. Emil Brunner, on the other hand, accepted both natural and special revelation. This latter position has been held by the Roman Catholic church.

4. *Models of Revelation* (New York: Doubleday & Co., 1983), pp. 36ff., chap. 3.

Revelation is also to be found in the history of biblical events.[5] H. Richard Niebuhr, in his near-classic book that makes this affirmation, calls the Bible the "book of the Acts of God" or the "drama of re-demption," which reveals God through the saving acts that formed and preserved the people of Israel through the settlement in Canaan by Abraham and his family, the sojourn in Egypt, the exodus and resettlement, kingdom, exile, and return.[6] Finally, the revelation of God is manifested in Jesus Christ and the birth of the Christian com-munity. The current emphasis on narrative theology continues this understanding of revelation.

Revelation is interpreted by some people as an inner experience.[7] For these the content of revelation is the experience of God. Recog-nizing that God is both transcendent and immanent, this approach to revelation emphasizes the immanence of God. This is the way of the mystics. Christian mysticism, however, as practiced for example by Teresa of Avila or Rufus M. Jones, is balanced by the recognition of the revelation of God in Scripture and in the life of the worshiping community.

Revelation may also be interpreted as dialectical presence.[8] Growing out of the theology of Karl Barth, who offered this as an "antidote" to revelation as inner experience, this affirms a tension between the transcendence and the immanence of God. God is known through God's own gracious action in the gift of faith. The revelation of who God is and how God acts is set forth in Scripture. But only faith reveals the history of the people of Israel and the life of Jesus Christ as the revelation of the transcendent God. This dialectical approach prevents viewing revelation either as propositional only or as an exclusively interior apprehension.

Revelation can also be understood as a new awareness.[9] Dulles presents Pierre Teilhard de Chardin as representative of this approach, citing his emphasis on knowing God from within.

A discussion of contemporary understandings of revelation would be incomplete without reference to the work of process theologians, which stems from the thought of Alfred North Whitehead and Charles Hartshorne. Leading exponents today are John B. Cobb, Jr., David Ray Griffin, and Marjorie Suchoki. The thesis of Cobb and Griffin is

---

5. Ibid., chap. 4, pp. 53ff.
6. *The Meaning of Revelation* (New York: Macmillan Co., 1960).
7. Dulles, *Models of Revelation,* chap. 5, pp. 69ff.
8. Ibid., chap. 6, pp. 84ff.
9. Ibid., chap. 7, pp. 98ff.

that "all activity is process." The world as we experience it is a place of process, of change, of becoming, of growth and decay.[10] They reject the distinction between natural and special revelation, viewing the wholeness of God's revelation in the natural world and in human experience, including history.[11] They describe God as "responsive and creative love."[12] Suchoki writes, "God's aim is God's adaptation of divine harmony to specific conditions in the world. What is actually seen as we observe the world is not the initial aim of God, but what has been done with that aim in the world's own dealing with it. In the dynamics of process, the influence of God is directional, orienting the occasion toward its best mode of being in the world."[13]

Ronald F. Thiemann is concerned to take the idea of revelation from a purely conceptual basis to a framework of "narrated promise." Revelation is seen within the context of God's prevenient grace and the human response. "Such a doctrine," he writes, "must maintain the distinction between divine initiative and human reception, while granting priority to the former."[14]

In conclusion it can be said that the Bible is the locus of God's special revelation. Through the Bible, in a unique way, people learn about God and are drawn to love and serve God. Revelation therefore includes the moral teaching through which people can know what obedience and commitment mean. Through the Bible the nature and activity of God are made known. Supremely for Christians, God, the Word of God, is made incarnate in Jesus Christ. In the words of Clark Pinnock, "the pattern of biblical revelation . . . includes propositional communication as well as personal communion. It presents the acts of God and the response of faith, the words of God and the call to obedience, the objective and the subjective. It tells us about God and it brings us to God."[15] Some understand God to be revealed through inner experience, while others see a dialectic between the experience of the transcendent and the immanent God. Revelation is also construed as conveying the awareness that brings fresh meaning into human life.

10. *Process Theology: An Introductory Exposition* (Philadelphia: Westminster Press, 1976), pp. 7, 14.

11. Ibid., p. 159.

12. Ibid., pp. 43-52.

13. *God, Christ, Church: A Practical Guide to Process Theology,* rev. ed. (New York: Crossroad, 1989), p. 41.

14. *Revelation and Theology* (Notre Dame, Ind.: University of Notre Dame Press, 1985), p. 96.

15. Clark H. Pinnock, *The Scripture Principle* (San Francisco: Harper & Row, 1984), p. 27.

AUTHORITY

The authority of the Bible lies in the belief of its writers—and its readers—that God is speaking through them and to them. It is authoritative in terms of the revelation: who God is, how God acts, and what God expects. Sally McFague, echoing Hans Georg Gadamer and Paul Ricoeur, writes that its authority for Christians lies in the kind of text Scripture is. "The authority of Scripture is the authority of a classic poetic text," she writes, and "such a notion of authority is substantial and enduring, both because *its authority is intrinsic* (the world it presents, that is, the reality it describes, speaks with power to many people across the ages) and because *its interpretation is flexible* (the world it presents is open to different understandings)."[16] The authority of the Bible, in this view, lies in its ability to speak to diverse people across the generations.

Clark Pinnock, from an evangelical perspective, describes the authority of the Bible as the book that testifies to salvation in Jesus Christ. He writes,

> The Bible is basically a covenant document designed to lead people to know and love God. As such, it has a focused purpose and concentration. This is the kind of truth it urges us to seek in it, and this is the context in which its truth claims ought to be measured. . . . Their treasure and their wisdom are oriented to presenting Jesus Christ, the wisdom and the power of God. We should never define biblical authority apart from this stated purpose or apply to it standards of measurement that are inappropriate.[17]

This last statement raises the question as to the areas of authoritativeness. One facet of this discussion is the issue of inerrancy, the idea that the Bible is without error.[18] This presupposes that the Bible is not only the Word of God but also the words of God, in effect a document written at divine dictation. Since God is by definition omniscient, to say otherwise would seem to strike at the basic understanding of who God is.

---

16. Sallie McFague. *Metaphorical Theology: Models of God in Religious Language* (Philadelphia: Fortress Press, 1982), p. 59.
17. *The Scripture Principle*, p. 55.
18. George M. Marsden, in *Understanding Fundamentalism and Evangelism* (Grand Rapids, Mich.: Wm. B. Eerdmans, 1991), discusses this issue in chapter 1, "The Protestant Crisis and the Rise of Fundamentalism," pp. 37-38.

Biblical scholar Donald Bloesch, however, calls for a more nuanced definition of the words *infallibility* and *inerrancy.* "When an absolute equation is made between the words of the Bible and the divine revelation," he writes, "the Word of God is placed in the power of men, since words and propositions can be mastered by reason. . . . I am not among those who wish to give up inerrancy and infallibility when applied to Scripture, but I believe that we need to be much more circumspect in our use of these and related terms. Scripture is without error in a fundamental sense, but we need to explore what this sense is."[19]

As we have seen in the previous chapter, the Bible grew from oral traditions to written documents and became collected into the books now regarded as Holy Scripture by a general consensus of the Christian community. Even when inspired, human beings are still fallible. The wonder of God's love is demonstrated in the power of the Scriptures to move people to know, love, and serve God generation after generation and in all corners of the earth. This is the response to the authority of Scripture as it reveals the nature and activity of God; relates the guidance of God in the history of Israel and at the beginnings of the church; proclaims God as Creator, Redeemer, Sanctifier; and records teachings that have guided individuals and nations in their personal and corporate lives.

INSPIRATION

This word comes from the Latin, *in spirare,* meaning "to breathe into." *Spirit* and *breath* are the same word in Hebrew. The Holy Spirit, then, is the "breath" of God. The word is used in Gen. 2:7: "then the Lord God formed man from the dust of the ground, and breathed into his nostrils the breath of life; and the man became a living being." The risen Jesus, appearing to the disciples, "breathed on them and said to them, 'Receive the Holy Spirit' " (John 20:22).

The meaning of the Holy Spirit as part of the trinitarian understanding of God is that God continues to be present and active in all the created world. To say that the Bible is inspired is to affirm that God's Holy Spirit guided those who acted and those who wrote. Diverse as the Bible is in its writings, and despite the wide span of

---

19. *The Future of Evangelical Christianity* (New York: Doubleday & Co.), 1983, p. 19.

time over which it was written, its essential unity lies in this affirmation: The Bible mediates the presence and activity of God through its pages.

But the action of the Holy Spirit through a person will always be limited by the ability of that person to hear and to interpret God's word, as every Christian knows. Human limitation is the questionable factor in any theory of verbal inspiration. Like the inerrancy or infallibility doctrines, this presupposes that God through the Holy Spirit has made it possible for humans to produce a perfect document. But Hans Küng suggests that the writing of Scripture "can be described as *Spirit-pervaded and Spirit-filled.* If—that is—the first witnesses think that they are moved by the divine Spirit, this will also determine their writing without having to prove to their hearers or readers that there is somewhere an act of inspiration which they must recognize. It is in fact simply taken for granted in the New Testament that every reception and proclamation of the Gospels happens *a priori* 'in the Holy Spirit.' "[20]

The inspiration of the Bible is what makes it "Holy" Scripture. The living God is revealed through its pages in the continuing action of God. But this inspiration must be matched by the action of the Holy Spirit in the reader if God is to be revealed to her or him. Many people read the Bible as a literary document, appreciating its qualities of poetry, drama, and chronicle. They may be drawn to the life of Jesus or impressed with the journeys of Paul. But they do not necessarily hear God speak to them as they read (although this is always a possibility). This is the meaning of the seemingly paradoxical statement that the Bible both *is* the Word of God and *becomes* the Word of God.

"All scripture is inspired by God and is useful for teaching, for reproof, for correction, and for training in righteousness" asserts one of the Pastoral Epistles (2 Tim. 3:16-17). This is not a mechanical idea of inspiration but simply the assurance that those who wrote were devoutly conscious of speaking for God.[21] The writer of 2 Peter recognizes the danger of dissension when every person becomes an interpreter, writing: "First of all you must understand this, that no prophecy of scripture is a matter of one's own interpretation, because no prophecy ever came by human will, but men and women moved

20. *On Being a Christian* (New York: Doubleday & Co., 1976), p. 465.
21. In *Beyond Fundamentalism: Biblical Foundations for Evangelical Christianity* (Philadelphia: Westminster Press, 1984), James Barr points out that the writers of this passage could not have been referring to the Bible that we have because the New Testament canon was not complete at that time (p. 4).

by the Holy Spirit spoke from God" (1:20, 21). Clearly the assertion of the inspiration of Holy Scripture has itself needed interpretation. Bernard Ramm's summary is helpful:

> Inspiration derives its life and substance from revelation. Revelation is prior in point of time to inspiration, and is the more important of the two doctrines. While it is the function of revelation to bring to the sinner a soteric knowledge of God, it is the function of inspiration to preserve that revelation in the form of tradition and then in the form of a *graphe*. That is to say, the specific function of inspiration is to *preserve revelation in a trustworthy and sufficient form*.[22]

Garrett Green links "image" and "imagination" in his book *Imagining God: Theology and the Religious Imagination*. The Inspiration of Scripture is "its imaginative force—its power to re-form and transform the human imagination, grounded in that 'secret act of God' that the New Testament calls the work of the Holy Spirit."[23] The image of God in which humans are made is a paradigm and this is the contact for revelation. God is revealed through the image of God, first at creation and now through Christ.

This leads to consideration of related scriptural doctrines of unity and authority, for Scripture then becomes the concrete paradigm. Thus Green speaks of the image becoming "impressed" on us through the scriptural narrative. "The divine-human point of contact can therefore be described as the faithful imagination, the human power to imagine, conformed to the image of God."[24] The unity of Scripture is to be found in its coherent pattern: its integrity, reliability, and the canon. He calls this the "shape of the mystery."[25]

The authority of the Bible is imaginative—that is, "Scripture, rightly employed, enables its hearers to imagine God." He concludes, "The Bible carries authority for the Christian community by embodying the classic paradigm of the Christian imagination. Scripture is the concrete exemplar in the life of the believing community, by which

---

22. *Special Revelation and the Word of God* (Grand Rapids, Mich. Wm. B. Eerdmans, 1962), pp. 175-76.
23. (San Francisco: Harper & Row, 1989), pp. 88-89).
24. *Imagining God: Theology and the Religious Imagination,* pp. 112-14.
25. Ibid., pp. 119, 123.

it is enabled to imagine God, and hence to imagine the world in its relation to God."[26]

In order to understand the use of the terms *imagination* and *imagine* in recent theological discourse, it is necessary to get beyond any notions of the imagination as the unreal, the unrealistic, and to see it as one avenue by which human beings can come to know and experience God and to understand Scripture. It means, as Walter Brueggemann and others have said, getting beyond the Cartesian insistence that the intellect—thinking—is the only key to knowing.

TRUTH AND FACT

The reliability of the Bible, for some people, hinges on the understanding of truth and fact. Facts are provable, or at least demonstrable. In this sense they are true. Facts can change from day to day. The weather report will vary; so will stock market quotations. These are statistics, valid for a specific time and place. Facts are frequently important. We emphasize this by saying, "That's a *fact*." The facticity of the Bible is important because Judaism and Christianity are historical religions. They can trace an ancestry through their communities of faith.

Facts are true. But not all truth is conveyed through facts. Indeed important truth can be embodied in other forms: story, poetry, drama, music, visual arts. Think of the power of a story such as Flannery O'Connor's "Displaced Person,"[27] which is uncomfortably suggestive of how Jesus would be treated were he to arrive among devout church people today. It is easier to read about him in the pages of the Gospel in a distant setting. Both narratives are true, but O'Connor's is fiction.

Or consider Francis Thompson's poem "The Hound of Heaven":

> I fled Him, down the nights and down the days;
> I fled Him, down the arches of the years;
> I fled Him, down the labyrinthine ways

---

26. The phrase *religious imagination* is basic to other recent writings, including David C. Bryant, *Faith and the Play of Imagination* (Macon, Ga.: Mercer University Press, 1989); John Bouker, *The Religious Imagination and the Sense of God* (Oxford: Clarendon Press, 1978); Gordon Kaufman, *The Theological Imagination* (Philadelphia: Westminster Press, 1981); David Tracy, *The Analogical Imagination: Christian Theology and the Culture of Pluralism* (New York: Crossroad, 1981); and, earlier, Amos Niven Wilder's brief and important *Theopoetic: Theology and the Religious Imagination* (Philadelphia: Fortress Press, 1976).

27. *Complete Stories* (New York: Farrar, Straus & Giroux, 1971), pp. 194-235.

Of my own mind.

It ends:

> Is my gloom, after all,
> Shade of His hand, outstretched caressingly?
> "Ah, fondest, blindest, weakest,
> I am He Whom thou seekest![28]

Whether autobiography or fiction, it speaks as directly to human experience as does any biblical narrative.

Biblical revelation and scriptural authority have the purpose of proclaiming truth as narrated in the story of Israel, of Jesus, and of the early Christian community.

Church historian Lester G. McAllister has written a history of the Christian Church, Disciples of Christ, and has also compiled a brief book of stories from that tradition. He titled the latter *Just Like I Heard It,* the answer a teller of tales would give when asked, "Is that so?" He writes: "Myths, legends, anecdotes, stories often may tell more of the truth than the facts. One of the difficulties of historical research is to separate the fact from the fiction. . . . We have a variety of stories, incidents, anecdotes and legends which are both fact and fiction and often it is difficult to separate the two. Some of the Disciples stories which are fiction tell a truth about ourselves more than a fact would."[29]

God is not bound by facts. Whatever medium draws people toward the saving love of God is a potential vehicle for revelation.

It is therefore not surprising that two versions of an event may vary, as in the history documented in 2 Kings and 2 Chronicles. The former originated in Israel; the latter tells the history of Judah.

The power of poetry may be demonstrated by reading each of the two stories of Deborah's victory over Sisera. Judges 4 is straightforward narrative. But Judg. 5:28, in vivid poetry, powerfully conveys the drama of the event by shifting focus briefly to Sisera's mother:

> "Out of the window she peered,
> the mother of Sisera gazed
> through the lattice:
> 'Why is his chariot so long in coming?

---

28. *Great Poems of the English Language* (New York: Tudor Publishing, 1933), p. 1115.
29. (Nashville: The Forrest F. Reed Lectures for 1988, Disciples of Christ Historical Society), p. x.

Why tarry the hoofbeats of his chariots?' "

Some would make a "harmonious" New Testament narrative by fitting together all four Gospels. This violates the intent of the writers, who, as was noted earlier with reference to the writers of Luke and John, chose their materials deliberately. All proclaim the good news in Jesus Christ, yet each wrote originally for a specific community of faith. Their differences are precious because they give us four portraits of Jesus, four dimensions. The epistles give us other dimensions as the first generation of Christians pondered the meaning of his life, death, resurrection, and continuing presence among them.

Hans Küng observes, "The story of what has actually happened . . . can leave us completely cold; on the other hand, we can occasionally be deeply moved by a made-up (fictitious) story of something that never happened historically. . . . These stories [in the Bible] were never meant to convey mere information, leaving the hearer or reader uninvolved. They contain a *message,* carrying with it a promise or a threat."[30]

The theologian Gabriel Fackre strongly affirms the primacy of narrative in the Bible, as is evident in the title of his book *The Christian Story: A Narrative Interpretation of Basic Christian Doctrine.* This is no traditional theological treatise. One might say that he uses the method of the Bible. He states, "A canonical narratologist holds that the truth conveyed [in biblical stories] is inseparable from the story form in which it comes to us. . . . In canonical story each of the features of narrative is seen to embody the very character of biblical faith, the open-endedness representing the freedom of both humanity and deity."[31]

Modern people are educated in a cognitive mold with an emphasis on scientific thinking and a sharp distinction between fact and the nonfactual, with the latter given less importance. Biblical fundamentalism, in stressing the facticity of the Bible, operates from the same presuppositions. Fundamentalist scholars believe that the Bible's every word must be proven factual in order for it to have credibility. Unfortunately, this approach alienates people at least as often as it convinces them.

People who are free to hear God speaking through different forms, by contrast, can respond through their feelings as well as their mind.

30. *On Being a Christian,* pp. 415 and 416.
31. Gabriel Fackre, *The Christian Story: A Narrative Interpretation of Basic Christian Doctrine* (Grand Rapids, Mich.: Eerdmans, 1985), p. 7.

The Psalms, for instance, tell the story of salvation with a dramatic simplicity that the historical section of the Bible lacks. These have been and continue to be moving expressions of faith for both personal and liturgical prayer. Parable was Jesus' preferred method of teaching. He did not lecture; he told stories and left people to identify with them where they would.

EXEGESIS/EXPOSITION

Exegesis is the technical interpretation of the Bible. The interpreter's work is colored by the presuppositions discussed in this chapter: the understanding of revelation, authority, and inspiration. An acceptance of the difference between truth and fact will influence the extent to which the various tools of research are employed. The exegete asks the questions, "What did this passage mean to the one who wrote it?" and "How was it expected to be understood by those who heard it?" In order to do exegesis, a person needs to know the nuances of the original language. Contemporary translations help even those with no knowledge of a language to know the variants of different manuscripts. It is also necessary to know something of the political and social setting in which the material was written. For example, understanding that Isaiah 1-39 was written during the existence of the kingdom of Judah and chapters 40-55 were written during the reign of Cyrus of Persia influences interpretation because the political setting of each was different.

Knowing something of the geographical setting is helpful. The patriarchal narratives take place in the arid area of the Negev. Most of the ministry of Jesus is placed in and around Galilean farming and fishing villages. The narratives are colored by their setting.

The exegete looks at the forms of the narrative: parable, legend, pronouncement story, poetry, teaching. These forms tell something about the biblical narrator and the audience.

Exegesis of the Hebrew Scriptures was taking place among the rabbis before the time of Jesus. One of the earliest modes was that of analogy and allegory. This was used even in the early twentieth century by some Christian exegetes, as seen in the introductions to the Song of Songs that interpret it as an allegory of Christ and the church. Modern exegesis has developed slowly along with the scholarly tools that have made it possible.

Hermeneutics is a term meaning "interpretation." It differs from exegesis in that it conveys the idea of principles of interpretation, and looks at the bases on which rest the exegesis of particular passages or books. It is the science of interpretation. Hermeneutics is the theoretical work; exegesis is the practical application.

Exposition, on the other hand, asks the question, "What does this Scripture passage say to people today? Exposition has been the preacher's approach. In its most thoughtful form, expository preaching begins with exegesis, which would include the use of biblical commentaries to illuminate the basic text. With the assumption that human nature does not change, even if the setting does, and that God still speaks through Scripture, the preacher tries to discern the text's relevance for the particular congregation. To "expose" the Scripture is not necessarily to give rules for living extracted from a passage. In a more lively way, exposition may retell the story so that listeners hear themselves addressed and seek to respond in their situation. Exposition is also used as a method of teaching in some adult Bible classes.[32]

VIOLENCE IN THE BIBLE

Violence is part of human life. The Bible begins with the murder of Abel by his brother Cain and ends with war in heaven. The light does not overcome the darkness easily.

Violence is endemic in film, television, and print. Inner-city churches and those in war-torn areas know firsthand what violence is and struggle to deal with the effects. They bring their experiences to the reading of the Bible. Compared to everyday reality, violence in the Bible is tame. Descriptions are sparse; the reader must supply the details. The problem is not the recounting of violence but the biblical assertion that God has ordained or commanded particular acts of violence.

The book of Numbers (chapter 16) recounts a revolt against the leadership of Moses led by the heads of three families and their followers. At the end, two of the leaders and their families are swallowed up by the earth. The next day all the people revolt, demanding a return to Egypt, and a plague comes upon them, stemmed only after great loss of life, when Aaron makes atonement on their behalf. Why, we ask, would a merciful God be so unjust as to command the destruction of the elders, women, and children along with the guilty men? Ancients

---

32. The Proclamation Series, published by Fortress Press and written by scholars and preachers, consists of brief volumes for each season of the church year and provides both exegesis and exposition of the Sunday texts for preachers and teachers.

did not have the same sense of individuality that modern Euro-Americans have. The family was a unit. In this perilous desert situation it was important to stem revolt. People today usually do not accept the decision of an inspired leader as necessarily the will of God.

A later story pits Saul against the last of the judges, Samuel (1 Samuel 15). Saul was ordered to destroy the Amalekites, but he spared their king and the best of the flocks. Saul explained that he had saved the cattle for sacrifice, but Samuel regarded them as booty (which Saul had been forbidden to take) and personally slew king Agag at the shrine at Gilgal. To Saul he said, "You have rejected the word of the Lord, and the Lord has rejected you from being king of Israel" (v. 26). This harsh judgment was the turning point in Saul's tragic life. The sin lay not in sparing the enemy king but in putting his judgment ahead of Samuel's, which was considered to be God's judgment. By any standard of war, neither the king's execution or Saul's rejection was unusual.

The so-called imprecatory psalms are hymns to God that may begin in praise and end pleading for the destruction of those causing the suffering of the suppliant or the nation—a very human response. "The wicked go astray from the womb. . . . They have venom like the venom of a serpent. . . . O God, break the teeth in their mouths; tear out the fangs of the lions, O Lord! . . . The righteous will rejoice when they see vengeance done" (Psalm 58, passim). These people did not hesitate to tell God exactly how they felt as they prayed. Their anguish caused their anger; their faith led them to believe that God would punish the wicked and avenge the righteous. Perhaps Christians are less honest in their prayers (as if God did not know the truth about each person). Seen in their context, these psalms can help adults deal with the anger felt in facing injustice to themselves and those they love.

Compare the crucifixion of Jesus in the Gospels with the novel *The Day Christ Died*, a recapitulation in detail hour by hour.[33] To the people who wrote and first heard the passion story, crucifixion was an everyday event all over the Roman empire, which had used this method for hundreds of years to execute common criminals. The Gospel writers' original audience did not need to hear the agonizing details; they needed to understand the meaning of Jesus' death. The cross, although a symbol of violence, has given strength and solace to Christians for centuries. It serves as a reminder of God's total participation in the suffering of humanity with redemptive power through Jesus. The

33. By Jim Bishop (New York: HarperCollins, 1991).

resurrection is unthinkable without the crucifixion. That is why the church celebrates the event with appropriate liturgies.

People need to believe that God is indeed just, and the affirmation of redemption, so powerfully enunciated through the Bible, gives this assurance to believers.

Violence is present in the Bible, but so is the constant refrain of the Creator's overarching love, the promise of redemption and restoration, the assurance that God is merciful and just. Millions are the victims of violence, but freedom given to humans in creation makes it possible for evil people to subvert the justice of God. Evil has human causes. There is no one theodicy to solve the perplexing human question of why God seems not to intervene to stem sin.

WHO INTERPRETS THE BIBLE?

The Roman Catholic Church is clear on this point. The documents of Vatican II consistently refer to the teaching office of the church, the magisterium. This is a responsibility to be taken with great seriousness. Believing scholars make up the teaching office and determine the boundaries of interpretation. Since Vatican II there has been more freedom for teaching scholars around the world to pursue their studies and publish the results. Yet reputed scholars are still occasionally silenced, and in recent years several have left their teaching positions at distinguished Catholic universities rather than submit to the interpretations required by church authorities. At its best, the affirmation that the church as a community shall have the final word in interpretation ensures a scholarly approach and maintains a certain harmony (or at least acceptance) within the whole community. But it can also become oppressive and can prevent the creative thinking and writing that often leads to valuable new insights.

The Protestant approach has sometimes gone to the other extreme, although the establishment churches of the Reformation have theological statements that set the boundaries of interpretation (the Westminster, Heidelberg, and Augsburg Confessions). These statements were the basis for occasional heresy trials of biblical professors early in the twentieth century when the fundamentalist-modernist struggle was developing. There are still clearly defined boundaries in fundamentalist seminaries, but considerably more freedom of interpretation is permitted in evangelical settings. In the educational institutions of the mainline denominations, as well as in ecumenical settings, a great deal of stimulating study and writing continues.

But some churches of the Protestant Reformation enunciated a doctrine allowing each person to interpret the Scriptures. This was a tradition within the Anabaptist groups, who differed from the mainstream churches in other ways, such as Baptism, the interpretation of the Lord's Supper, forms of worship, polity, and, frequently, lifestyle. Their distinctiveness was based on their interpretations of the Bible. Here too it could be said that the church as a gathered congregation was defining the boundaries of interpretation.

The centuries since the Reformation have witnessed the proliferation of Christian denominations and communities. Groups within congregations have differed and split. The divisions continue today as Christians clash over interpretations of Scripture affecting lifestyle, moral issues and the ordination of women.

Perhaps there will never be a balance between the interpretation of a particular church community and that of all its members. Holding to a center while permitting individual dissent requires a liberal spirit. The pain arises at the point where the whole seems threatened by the dissolution of the parts.

Also involved in the question of who interprets the Bible is the place of the clergy as interpreters. In most denominations the clergy have had graduate theological education in a school that mirrors the interpretations of the denomination that ordains them and usually of the parish in which they find themselves. But so diffuse, and even neglected, is biblical study within most parishes that it is possible for the minister to have one approach to biblical interpretation, the Sunday school teacher(s) another, and church members a third. The curriculum materials, whatever their orientation, will be taught through the teacher's interpretation. Frequently the pastor does not know what material is being taught.

Perhaps the best answer to who interprets the Bible would be to suggest a basic consistency of approach coupled with flexibility for those who teach. Without serious Bible study by a number of people in the congregation, the biblical Word can have little influence on the life of the congregation or its individual members.

IMPLICATIONS FOR CHRISTIAN EDUCATION

Matters of biblical interpretation affect all who are involved in the educational work of the church: teachers, parents, and clergy; laypeople and professionals. They need to think through these basic theological issues and come to a personal understanding of how they themselves interpret revelation, authority, and inspiration and how this relates to their work as teachers.

They need to develop a deep understanding of the revelatory work of God through Scripture: that God is speaking to them and to those whom they teach, reaching out to them, calling them to respond to God's love in their life. This personal understanding will help them to realize that they are channels for the revelation of God. Through them learners will be enabled to respond to God.

When teachers have come to an understanding of the authority of the Bible, they will be able to teach authoritatively. This sense of being called and given words to speak elicits confidence in those who learn and gets their attention. The teacher is one who continues to learn but who presumably is somewhat farther along the path.

Aware that the Holy Spirit gave words to those from whom we have the Scriptures, teachers will feel confident that God is continually leading and instructing them through the Holy Spirit. Through continuing prayer and Bible study, they will develop increasing confidence that they can help others interpret the biblical Word for their lives.

As they think seriously about the role of "truth" and "fact" in the Bible, teachers will develop a freedom to enjoy the many forms that truth takes and will be able to teach with confidence. They will not be disturbed about possible conflicts between the learners' worldview and the biblical worldview. They will come increasingly to understand both the particularity and the universality of the Bible. God speaks to all people in all places, because in the witness of the Bible the transcendent one dwells among human beings, even taking on humanity in Jesus. This is both fact and truth. The story is told in many forms.

Teachers will develop exegetical skills by using commentaries. They will find an atlas, a Bible dictionary, and a concordance helpful in their personal learning as well as in teaching. Teachers will become careful about the way they use exposition so that they do not distort the Bible. They will develop flexibility to allow learners to explore their own answers to the question, "What is the Bible saying to me?

Teachers will look critically at the curriculum materials available to them for teaching and grasp the underlying understandings about revelation, authority, inspiration, and especially about the way in which these materials deal with both truth and fact. Materials that take all of the Bible literally fail to realize its teaching potential for involving the whole person. In this way all who teach—pastors, parents, teachers—become better equipped for their calling.

Methods of
Bible Study

KNOWING THE BACKGROUND FOR BIBLICAL STUDY is important.
This gives teachers (who may also be pastors or parents) a foundation
from which to teach. You now know the literary development that
has shaped the biblical writings. You know the fundamentals from
which the Scriptures are interpreted. You understand why the Bible
is basic to Christian education.

But this will not enable you to interact with a class in such a way
that people will learn. You need methods for teaching. In a broad
sense, any method can be used with any age level, but it will need to
be adapted. Whether the learners are preschoolers or adults, teachers
will envision ways to use a particular method to the best advantage
with that age group.

STORY

Primary learning comes through stories. Children are told stories
almost as soon as they can understand connected speech from the
adults around them. They are given books with a simple story line.
They hear narrative descriptions of experience. Adults use stories almost without realizing it. Conversation at every social gathering includes the recounting of anecdotes. Sermons include illustrative material in story form. Some preachers say they could repeat a sermon
to the same congregation a year later if they changed the illustrations.
People would remember the illustrations but not the surrounding
didactic material.

This may lead you to think that excellent storytelling has characterized this method when used for religious education. Unfortunately this is not so. Look at the Bible stories provided in curricular materials for preschool children. They are usually too brief to include any drama. A story must involve the hearers by making vivid the plot, its development, and its characters.[1] Because the attention span of a preschool child is assumed to be brief, Bible stories are written with brevity as a criterion. When children are conditioned to the split-second timing of their lively television programs, it is assumed that they will not listen. This is not so when the teacher telling a story dramatizes it, keeps eye contact with the hearers, and uses voice and body language for emphasis. A story is not a recital of facts but an involvement in people and events. Hearers live the story to which they are listening. They become involved, and it speaks to them.

Story is certainly the most used mode of teaching for younger elementary children, but here again religious education material is usually briefer and less vivid than are equivalent stories that boys and girls read in school and at home. A number of Bible storybooks exist to enrich and supplement the "story of the week." Cassettes alone or in conjunction with books add another dimension to story telling.

With older elementary children, the story, again told briefly, is often the only basis for discussion. Learners are invited to view the Bible cognitively and answer questions of content for clarification or for meaning. This can be considered a use of story, but it again ignores the primary value of story: to make the listener part of the narrative. Older boys and girls are reading books that absorb them in the lives and situations of others their own age or of adults whose lives have made a difference. But few biblical books or stories are sufficiently well written to absorb the concentration of those who love to read. The heroines and heroes of the Bible, called by God, flawed yet faithful, are all too seldom the reading fare of young Christians.

Stories are seldom found in curricular outlines designed for adolescent studies. Caught up in the idea that this is a time for abstract operational thinking, religious education materials concentrate on life experiences, paying more attention to presenting a situation than to portraying it vividly. These seek to use biblical teaching to assist in decision making, a necessary task. But life situations can be told in story form so that hearers become participants and decisive situations

---

1. The public library can supply you with good books on storytelling, some specifically written for religious education. Look for tapes that demonstrate the techniques.

come closer to reality. The life stories of biblical people raise ethical questions similar to those young people are asking today.

Religious educator Locke Bowman writes

> It seems, then, that we should ask—for young people in the Church—that they be told the story of Moses in such a way that it will strike them as a significant meeting between God and a person destined to make a profound difference in the world. We would hope they could know Moses in conjunction with their learning that God speaks and acts for the good of humankind. In each new generation, the telling of the story must be done lovingly and sensitively, with great reverence for the truth it reveals. We hardly need ask more of the church's teachers than faithfulness to the scriptural account, coupled with a very special concern for every learner. We then trust that the result will be a partial but foundational knowledge; the way must be left open for new and lively encounters with Moses in the ensuing years of each child's life.[2]

Adult classes can be the most traditional ones in a congregation. They may consist of a biblical passage, a set of questions about the meaning, and concluding discussion questions applying the passage to life. But newspapers, periodicals, and television are filled with narrative material. Adults read novels, and short stories are staple reading fare. The deliberate use of the Bible in narrative form has been forgotten. Story, we seem to say, is for children. Not so. We are these people: Sarah, David, Peter, Martha, but we do not recognize this when the biblical stories are presented as didactic material. The teaching methods used have enabled adults to stand outside the story and observe the people in order to learn from them lessons on how to live the Christian life. The teaching of adults is weakened when teachers are not given tools with which they can help learners identify with those who so long ago were called by God and followed with whatever faithfulness they could muster.

Frederick Houk Borsch, a biblical scholar and Episcopal bishop, compares stories to art:

> The audience is also invited to wonder about more than can be told because the life the artist is seeking to represent is so often

---

2. *Teaching for Christian Hearts and Minds* (San Francisco: Harper 1990), pp. 2-3.

problematic and mysterious. Not everything can be clearly stated, because not everything is understood or known. The faithful story also conveys that awareness, at the same time trying to intimate more than can otherwise be said. Such stories do not so much comprehend an insight as try to penetrate more deeply into what is experienced—or even seems just about to be experienced—but cannot be clearly articulated. The hearer is invited to probe in that direction.[3]

The mode of teaching often used by Jesus was story—parables. Understanding how to approach parables is important for teaching them. As readers are reminded in Borsch's book, and especially in the writings of John Dominic Crossan, parables are stories to be entered into, and when we do this we will be made uncomfortable by the roles we are playing. Parables are meant to disturb.

Story is basic to Scripture. The Bible contains the story of God's gracious action through the people of Israel and of the Christian community. Read it and see how vividly the story is told. The narratives are brief and do not elaborate settings or characters except where this is necessary for the action. But the drama is there, sometimes in only a word or a phrase. All Bible stories in curricular materials—for whatever age level—need to be checked against the biblical text itself. You may be surprised at how retellers can unintentionally distort the Bible. In their attempts to make a story shorter, they often lose its emotional impact. To make it longer they imagine details and miss the artistry of the biblical writers.

Hans-Ruedi Weber reminds us that Scriptures were meant to be recited.[4] Widespread literacy is a modern phenomenon. Even the invention of printing did not give most people access to the Bible, although it did make the Bible more widely available to churches, to groups who wanted to gather for Bible study, and to the educated elite.

Even though most people in today's congregations can read, Weber reminds us that the Bible must be heard. Today cassette recorders help that process by permitting people to tape readings and then to discuss them. His advice:

In order for the biblical message to be heard it must be told well. Biblical communicators must therefore learn not only how to

---

3. *Many Things in Parables: Extravagant Stories of New Community* (Philadelphia: Fortress Press, 1988), p. 3.
4. Chap. 2, "Hearing God's Message," p. 12.

preach a Sunday sermon, but also how to tell a story. An important part of this learning process is to become sensitive to poetry, for much of biblical theology appears in the form of "theopoetics." Just as form and content are intimately related in poetry, so the biblical message cannot be abstracted from its manifold forms. It must be told and heard as a message through stories and proverbs, through parables and letters, through prayers, confessions, and visions.[5]

Storytelling is an art that requires practice. The teller must know the content of the story, identify with it, and learn to tell it dramatically. Fortunately books on the subject today include illustrative tapes so those learning how to tell a story can hear a model. Story reading also requires practice, for the reader must be free from dependence on the text and be able to include drama through the voice and with gestures.

The Bible text itself should be read more often simply for its own impact. Brief books such as Ruth and Jonah can be read in such a way that hearers identify with the people and understand the message from inside. The Gospel of Mark, only sixteen chapters, can involve a congregation powerfully through those first disciples who were witnesses to the life, death, and resurrection of Jesus. These stories are not age-graded. An intergenerational congregation for an evening service or a church supper can listen appreciatively. Reading the full text would be an effective way to study one of these books with a class. How to narrate it is suggested by religious educator Donald E. Miller:

> In telling a story the storyteller stands in the framework of the story. Questioning is suspended for the moment. The narrative becomes an expression of the teller. The interest of the story depends more upon the teller's total identification with the story than upon the story's being totally comprehensible.
>
> At the same time, the storyteller has a certain distance from the story. The storyteller knows that this is a special time, "storytime." The storyteller is responsive to signals from the listeners, and anticipates their point of view.[6]

---

5. Ibid., p. 17.
6. *Story and Context: An Introduction to Christian Education* (Nashville: Abingdon, 1987), p. 117.

The reason that biblical stories appeal to a wide range of ages is that so often they depict feelings and situations that everyone experiences: love, fear, anger, sin, forgiveness, restoration. The story of the Bible is history, but more intimately it is the life of each individual touched by God. It is important to remember, especially in dealing with the Gospels, that we are human. We are not Jesus, healing and saving, but rather the disciples, the critics, the sick and the sinful who meet him and are confronted by him. How did they respond? How would we respond?

Weber acknowledges the great strides in biblical interpretation that have come through opportunities to study the Bible in technical ways. But he stressed the need to get beyond the limitations inherent in "the Bible as a printed book." As such, he writes, it

> appeals far more to the human intellect than to human emotion and imagination. The very term "Bible study" is a child of a literary culture in which the capacity for meditation and celebration often remains underdeveloped. Also the tendency to individualism and privacy can be fostered by the printed book: each one has his or her own Bible to read and explain as one wishes. The actual degree of participation in the biblical drama together with God's people of biblical times and of our time remains low."[7]

He urges us not to concentrate so much on the left side of the brain (the rational) but to encourage the development of the right side (the intuitive understanding), and to do this as members of the believing community.

DRAMA

Drama is closely allied with story. In India the sacred stories, the *Mahabharata* and the *Ramayana,* are frequently told as drama, pantomime, and dance. The Christian use of drama began in the Middle Ages with simple depictions of the nativity, the Passion, and the resurrection acted out in the chancel during the liturgical celebration of these events. As religious education, these were more dynamic than pictorial representations of biblical events.

---

7. *Experiments in Bible Study,* p. 11.

Today religious drama takes many forms. Participants may respond informally to the reading of a biblical story by assuming roles and replaying it in their own words. This is a way of participating in the story, identifying with biblical people, and understanding both their actions and our responses. More formally, a biblical book or passage can be arranged for drama by highlighting roles with direct speech and providing continuity through a narrator. This is used today in a liturgical setting on Good Friday, when the passion story is read and the congregation becomes the crowd. It is a shocking experience to speak aloud words that Christians assume they would never say: "Crucify him!" The Psalms can be recited dramatically, in choral form, using voices of different timbres and noting the places where a unison response is indicated.

Playwrights have occasionally concerned themselves with religious drama: Noah, Gideon, Job, and Jonah have been the subject of plays where interpretation has enriched the hearer's understanding of the biblical text. These can be given formal treatment with costumes and settings or can be done effectively through playreading.[8]

The passion play, formally presented, has a long tradition. Oberammergau's may be the longest continuing one, but there are several places in the United States where it is an annual event to which people come from a distance. Here the events from Palm Sunday through the resurrection and ascension are dramatized with music and choir and a large cast.

Music and drama are combined in some expressions of the biblical story. Benjamin Britten's *Noye's Fludde,* taking a few liberties in depicting Noah's family, puts human drama into the story. Even the youngest children get into the act masked as animals entering the ark two by two singing *Kyrie eleison* and exiting at the close with "Hallelujah!" This is designed as chancel drama.

Popular music has brought two biblical stories to the professional stage, and these are now becoming known among church groups. *Godspell,* a musical based on the Gospel according to Matthew, has so popularized its hymn tunes that some of the new music is as familiar now as the traditional melodies, such as "All Good Gifts" and "Day by Day."[9] *Joseph and the Amazing Technicolor Dreamcoat,* originally written for performance in the private school attended by the composer's son, is now used by many church youth groups, who thereby learn

---

8. Books are available in local libraries to help people use informal and less structured approaches to presenting drama than is required by an elaborate production.

9. Music and new lyrics (for the recording) by Stephen Schwartz.

one version of the Bible story while they enjoy the fun of theatrical production.[10] It is to be hoped that they begin by reading the original and then take the opportunity to discuss the musical as commentary. *Jesus Christ Superstar* is a biblical musical published in 1970.[11]

The involvement of the listener in a musical is not as intense as in drama, where the person is more completely drawn into the emotional situation. But its form of commentary has value. *Joseph and the Amazing Technicolor Dreamcoat* ("technicolor" suggests an approach) is a refreshing change from the sometimes dull seriousness of the Sunday school version. *Godspell* insistently draws the viewer to the central character.

Film is another form of drama. Cecil B. deMille's *Ten Commandments* (1923) was an early interpretation, characteristic of film interpretation in its time. Films are easily and inexpensively available on videotape for showing in small groups as well as at larger assemblies. The life of Jesus has been the focus of quite a few films. Pasolini's *The Gospel according to Saint Matthew* catches the constant teaching activity of the story. The controversial *Last Temptation of Christ* is compelling in its depiction of one driven by his vocation, God-possessed and faithful. *Jesus of Montreal* uses the device of a passion play to ask how Jesus would fare in a modern city. Each of these, seen in connection with a reading of the Gospel, can be a powerful focus for asking, Who do you say that I am?

Some films are Gospel oriented without being directly biblical. *Babette's Feast* is an example—a wonderful story of the gratitude of the stranger and the odd discomfort with which it is received.

Drama in its many forms is a lively teaching method because the viewers are involved. They cannot take a "balcony" view, looking at the biblical story in an objective way. They must respond as one experiencing those events. To fully appreciate the possibilities of drama, viewers need to be prepared by reading the relevant biblical materials in advance, and they need to talk about them afterward. Although it is useful to view a production critically, viewers must not use this to avoid questions about where they stand and how they are responding.

VISUAL ARTS

Social scientist H. Marshall McLuhan, in writing about the post-Gutenberg era, observed that the print orientation that had served so

---

10. Andrew Lloyd Webber and Tim Rice.
11. Andrew Lloyd Webber and Tim Rice.

well for education and communication since the sixteenth century no longer held first place.[12] People were responding more fully to pictorial modes of knowing. Radio was being displaced by television; books by film. The thesis was explored extensively in the world exposition staged at Montreal in 1968 and succeeding world expositions. This trend is evident in the introduction to science enjoyed by multitudes at Epcot Center in Florida. The church has been slow to explore this avenue of education fully.

Early visual presentations of biblical events may be found in the catacomb drawings in Rome, dating from the second century. (The biblical ban on graven images precluded such drawing in Jewish contexts.) These simple line drawings in Christian burial places included Christ the good shepherd, a eucharistic meal, Moses, Daniel, Jacob's dream, the Virgin and child, Jonah, and the Samaritan woman. The biblical stories were well known.

When Christians could build churches, after Constantine's Edict of Toleration in 315, places of worship were ornamented with depictions of biblical stories. The churches of Ravenna in Italy, dating from the fifth and sixth centuries, are a treasure trove of biblical art. San Apollinare Nuovo (525) contains wonderful scenes from the life of Christ, saints, and prophets. San Vitale (527–47) is similarly decorated, as is San Apollinare in Classe (549). The twelfth-century Cathedral of Monreale near Palermo in Sicily continued the Byzantine tradition in both its architecture and its biblical art. Renaissance Italy saw a flowering of artistic expression. Veronese, Titian, Raphael, and Michelangelo expressed the faith of that time in opulent canvases that placed biblical events in Italian settings. Rembrandt is uniquely an artist of the Reformation in the starkness of his biblical portrayals. Twentieth-century art is expressed in quite different forms. People accustomed to representational art find it difficult to interpret Chagall's biblical paintings. Liturgical art and religious art are distinguished by their setting and use. A Titian painting at the back of an altar is liturgical art. In a monastic refectory it is religious art.

In a culture attuned to the movement of film and television, a picture or a photo is a specialized and seemingly less lively medium. Yet museums are thronged with viewers and spend large sums of money on selected exhibits. An El Greco exhibit displayed in Toledo, Ohio, and Toledo, Spain, was an education in the theology of the Counter-Reformation (with explanatory material by John W. Cook of Yale University). Any Rembrandt exhibit will be filled with biblical art.

---

12. The book setting forth the thesis is *The Gutenberg Galaxy: The Making of Typographic Man* (Toronto: University of Toronto Press), 1962.

The church has been slow to use this wealth of biblical art. Good reproductions should be found in each classroom, meeting room, and corridor. The pictures need only the explanatory labeling an art museum would give. Art can be used as a method of teaching a biblical course. A study of Mark's Gospel using art from a variety of periods can challenge participants to compare the artist's vision with the biblical words and to explore the interpretations. Usually these will mirror the theology of that time; sometimes they represent a personal viewpoint.

Traditional Sunday school pictures have appealed more to the mind than to the emotions. Their attempts to re-create a biblical setting and to depict children in supposed Palestinian dress are really no more realistic than the interpretations of fine artists are. Much of the present material in curriculum teaching packets is couched in the idiom of children's book illustration—not cartoon style but a generic depiction that may enable a wider range of viewers to identify with the characters. These are for immediate and temporary use, to illustrate a story or to encourage conversation. They do not draw the viewer in the same way that the fine artist's vision can. Children need both kinds of pictures.

Photos are a powerful form of art because of the immediacy they bring to the subject. For obvious reasons they can't depict biblical scenes. But they can show the topographical situation of the Bible—desert and wilderness, mountain, lake and river, city and countryside. These help readers to visualize the setting for biblical stories: the road to Jericho, the Negev, the fertile farmland of Galilee, a Herodian fortress. They help to interpret allusions in the Psalms: "I lift my eyes to the hills" suggest the approach to Jerusalem (Ps. 121:1); "desert into pools of water" (Ps. 107:35) reflects the change from the dry to the rainy season. Slide shows or videotapes made from such photos can enrich teaching.

Liturgical art is a study in itself. The forms of the altar cross or crucifix have varied across the centuries and express faith in the redeeming Christ. Tortured figures tell of the pain of medieval years; empty crosses symbolize the resurrection. Chalices and other articles used for the liturgy have always been lovingly and beautifully made. Editions of the Bible are specially prepared for liturgical use, as are service books. Windows tell the biblical story. Icons are the glory of the Eastern Orthodox faith, which shuns realistic representation of sacred figures and reverences them in their traditional stylized form. Symbols adorn churches—of God, of the Trinity, of the apostles. These represent meaning in a condensed form. The windows also tell the story, often in the glorious tones of stained glass.

The visual approach must include archaeological artifacts. Those who are near museums know that docents are available by pre-arrangement to guide groups through sections depicting the lands of the Bible, not only the Holy Land but Egypt, Assyria, Persia, Greece, and Rome. A few theological seminaries have such collections, and traveling kits of archaeological artifacts exist. You may not want to go so far as to organize a neighborhood dig in order to demonstrate how archaeology is done, but the archaeology of ancient America is being studied in many places and a visit to a site by a group would give them an idea of the process by which biblical history is being uncovered.

LEARNING THROUGH MUSIC

Music for praise and thanksgiving is part of the biblical experience, attested to in the Psalms and in descriptions of celebrations. Miriam, tambourine in hand, led the women in praising God for the safe delivery from Egypt (Exod. 15:20-21). David's music soothed a troubled king. The early Christians were admonished "with gratitude in your hearts sing psalms, hymns, and spiritual songs to God" (Col. 3:16). The use of music in the Bible is a study in itself. The Psalms have been called the hymnal of the Bible.

Hymnals today explore the range of Christian hymnody from the fourth century to the present day. As early as Ambrose of Milan's "O Splendor of God's Glory Bright" (fourth century) hymns in praise of Christ can be matched to all the names ascribed to him in the New Testament. One rich source of hymnody is the Advent-Epiphany season, beginning with "O Come, O Come, Emmanuel" (ninth century), with its images from the Old Testament, and Charles Wesley's "Come, Thou Long-Expected Jesus," with its roots in the prophets. This is succeeded by the Passion-Easter cycle, which begins with Theodore of Orleans, "All Glory, Laud, and Honor" (ninth century), and includes "The Day of Resurrection" by John of Damascus (eighth century) with its references to our Christian roots in Passover. Psalms paraphrases were part of the Reformed tradition, the best known being "All People That on Earth Do Dwell" from Psalm 100 by William Kethe (seventeenth century). You can explore your own hymnal to find the riches that will enhance your study of the Bible.

Contemporary themes and music will be found in new hymnals and in alternative hymnals published by denominational or independent sources. British writer Brian A. Wren has written popular hymns for every season of the liturgical year that are always sensitive to the social dimension of the Christian witness. The new hymnals often feature hymns from Asian and African Christians and Native American and African American hymns. "Were You There When They Crucified My Lord?" has become a basic hymn for Good Friday.

Mainstream denominations have largely deleted nineteenth-century gospel hymns from the repertoire, but today gospel is a popular form of music, and gospel singers make headlines. Strongly biblical in motifs and basic to the music of African American congregations, gospel is finding a place in congregations that include informal liturgies and in other group settings.

The concern for inclusive language has led to revisions in recently published hymnals. "Good Christian Friends Rejoice" does not change the meaning of that Christmas hymn, but it does include women and children. Some congregations using older hymnals suggest substitute words in the bulletin. Others use bulletin inserts as a way of introducing new hymns and inclusive language.

The liturgical churches have canticles and biblical responses that punctuate the service. The monastic custom of chanting continues. In the Anglican tradition, this is retained in sung Morning Prayer and in Evensong, Plainsong, Anglican chant, and modern chants designed for the contemporary English of recent service books are a mode between singing and saying that evokes a meditative way of hearing and saying Scripture.

One of the glories of biblical expression in song is found in the cantatas of Johann Sebastian Bach. These were written specifically for the lectionary Scripture of each Sunday in the church year. The moving power of Bach lies in his understanding of the biblical theology that both his music and the words express. A choir and congregation would have their spiritual life deepened by studying and participating in the performance of cantatas and joining together in the chorales. With excellent recordings available, a particular cantata can be selected either to introduce or to conclude a unit of biblical study.

Oratorios, being much longer compositions, would be unsuitable for a Sunday service. These are concert pieces, frequently used at special services. They retell the biblical story in narrative, recitative, solo, and chorus. The best known is Handel's *Messiah*. A choir preparing this, or a congregation that will hear it, could follow the biblical references for a better understanding of what the composer intends.

How does the music fit the words? Note the context of the texts. Trace the story as Handel tells it.

The two great Bach Passions, St. Matthew and St. John, are powerful expressions of the meaning of the event and vivid portrayals of the people involved. The listener cannot easily stand outside the story, although thousands of people listen to concert performances each year, many of them uninvolved in any religious faith. The chorales are commentary on the human involvement in the crucifixion of the Lord. "'Tis I whose sin now binds thee. . . . 'Tis I should bear it, I alone" (St. Matthew Passion), and the concluding chorale of the St. John Passion, frequently sung by the audience joining the chorus: "Lord Jesus Christ, O hear thou me, Thy Name I praise eternally!"

The passion theme has haunted composers from Buxtehude's austere classicism to the tortured modernity of Prenderecki. The contemporary composer sees the agony of the crucifixion but lacks the affirmation of the resurrection that Bach reflects. Discerning students can explore these differences in theological meaning, comparing Handel and Bach, for example.

Christmas music is another rich source for biblical interpretation. Berlioz's "Infancy of Christ" focuses on the visit of the Magi and the consequent anxiety of the holy family's flight into Egypt. Bach's Christmas cantata is celebratory.

Here, as in art, a distinction needs to be made between liturgical and religious music. Liturgical music is designed for use as part of a service of worship, including choir anthems, although frequently today such music is performed in a concert setting. Religious music is designed to be heard in a concert setting. Bernstein's "Chichester Psalms" or Poulenc's "Gloria" might be examples.

CREATIVE EXPRESSION AND THE BIBLE

The methods of Bible teaching explored thus far have been those by which learners become involved in the experience and expression of another person, participating in or identifying with literature, art, or music. In this way they can find deeper ways of experiencing the Bible and become strengthened in their own faith and knowledge. Another related approach allows students to express through these mediums what they themselves have learned about the Bible.

Storytelling is an example. Children are asked to retell a Bible story they have heard either to affirm the accuracy of their hearing or, a week later, to review the story. People at any age level may be asked to do this, interpreting the setting and the characters as they do so. Their interpretations are then discussed with reference to the story the Bible tells. Where there is more than one version, this discovery leads to discussion about the variants. Participants may be asked to tell the story in a modern setting, which will help them interpret what the Bible says to our time.

Drama is another example. In planning this form of retelling a biblical story, a group indicates how they will interpret it. Tone of voice and body language will reveal their attitude toward the characters. They are not simply identifying with the story; they are interpreting it. This can be seen, for instance, when members of the congregation read the Sunday lessons. Each reader indicates a personal understanding of the passage by the way he or she reads aloud. Learners are further encouraged in creativity when asked to develop a modern parallel to a passage. Whether performed spontaneously or carefully worked out in print, this requires serious consideration of the meaning of Scripture in contemporary terms.

Children often draw pictures of a Bible story they have just heard. But visual expression is not for children only. Every picture is an interpretation. Adolescents and adults can make graphic interpretations in their own manner. These might be drawings, cartoon figures, or an assemblage of newspaper headlines as commentary. Film and videotape are so widely used today that a learning group of almost any age might find these creative vehicles for expressing and interpreting biblical material.

An understanding of the background and historical flow of the Bible can be learned through the study and making of maps, time lines, and models. Charts outline a book. Classrooms from kindergarten through university and business conference rooms are filled with such visual aids to learning. Many churches are bare of these learning tools.

Verse is the most neglected form of teaching. Unrhymed verse is a way of responding emotionally to a passage. Poetry—from the Psalms to contemporary works—gives suggestions. Haiku is a promising form because of its simple structure. It comprises three lines totaling seventeen syllables—5-7-5.

You may think of music as too technical to be a useful form of creative expression of the Bible. Some people have this skill and should be encouraged. Yet others may want to write words to go with hymn tunes. This differs from free poetry in that the meter must match that of the hymn tune chosen.

Spontaneity is the key. Although these methods are used in teaching children, who seem unself-conscious when expressing themselves in various mediums, we sometimes hesitate to go beyond merely verbal exercises with adolescents and adults. This is curious, because today television, film, radio, and cassette (the ever-present Walkman) are commonplace. Teachers need to explore ways of using these mediums creatively in the classroom.

Passages in the Prophets, the wisdom literature, and the epistles are not stories. These need to be interpreted in verbal or visual forms that give concrete expression to their meaning. Modern proverbs, poems, prophetic words for this day, or letters to Christian churches here help participants reflect on the contemporaneity of the ancient forms. How would a prophet speak today? Write a "letter to the editor" in response to a prophet's message. Reflect on the prophet's words in the form of a meditation or prayer.

Discussion can be a creative method of teaching. The Bible needs to be interpreted if its meaning is to be discerned for us and our time. Walter Brueggemann has an interesting interpretation of the teaching method of Torah. He points out that the children ask the questions, and the parent answers. He quotes Exod. 12:26: "And when your children say to you, 'What do you mean by this service'? you shall say . . ." These answers are authoritative (but not authoritarian) because they represent the community and bind the generations together. He contrasts this with our catechetical methods in which the teacher asks the questions.[13] He further notes that this teaching is done within a liturgical setting (worship as pedagogy). He adds,

> In contrast to humanistic education, this mode of education does not assume that the child must locate a normative answer in his or her own experience, as though immediate experience yielded credo insights on the spot. Children are not expected to do this in Israel because normative articulations of faith are not individual, private conjurings. Moreover, in contrast to the catechetical tradition in which children memorize the right answer and parrot it back, the role of the child here is openness and wonderment. Nothing about the exchange is heavy or dictated. This should stimulate considerable thought, since so much church education

13. *The Creative Word: Canon as Model for Biblical Education* (Philadelphia: Fortress Press, 1982).

has bounced back and forth between heavy catechetical instruction imposed on the learners and privatized faith in which persons are pressed to be authors of their own faith.[14]

The use of questions is a subtle area of methodology. Carefully structured questions cause teacher and learner to probe together the depths of meaning, both to the original writers of the biblical text and to the people who today read and affirm it as the basis for their life. Discussion flows from this creative use of questions. Discussion requires openness on the part of all involved: a freedom to express their disagreements and doubts as well as to affirm their agreement. Elder Brewster's much-quoted statement is important: "God has still new light to break forth from his holy Word." Discussion represents one of the arts of teaching.

COMPUTERS

Many forms of technology have been used for teaching the Bible. The printing press, enabling the widespread dissemination of books, is such a form. Currently videotape is proving to be simple and useful. The computer is the next wave in biblical learning tools. Those who attend professional meetings know that there are many companies selling software programs for scholarly research: texts, concordances, and biblical languages. Computers are widely used in homes, where both children and adults compose cards and letters, create graphics and art, and play games. Many schools have classroom computers or computer rooms and make instruction available to students.

Computer resources for congregational Bible study have been slower in coming. When churches first buy a computer, they use it to keep mailing lists and financial records. Locked in the office, it is unavailable for religious education, although most people now know how to use a computer and would gladly do so at church if the right programs were obtained.

Computers are useful in teaching facts. Because they are emotionally neutral (as a teacher is not perceived to be), they can correct in a positive way and make it easy for the student to learn at an individual pace. Learning the content is a prerequisite to any serious discussion of meaning. Bible teaching has too often been strong on discussion without basic content. The computer can also be used for review and

14. Ibid., pp. 17-18.

drill. Its strength lies in the fact that it encourages accuracy, specific learning, and individual results. The student may use the computer before class begins or at any time during the session, for it is not usually intrusive in sight or sound. It works best in a learning center environment, where learners are engaged in varied but individual tasks. Two can use a program together, but the use of the keyboard limits the number. The computer can suggest questions for understanding that grow out of the content, but these would need to be pursued in a larger group setting.

Computers can also be used, as they are at home, for games. Many Bible game software programs are technological variants of long-played Bible games. Others offer simulations, which depict biblical situations on screen.

Biblical software programs are needed, and, fortunately, more are being developed by companies that specialize in them.[15] Congregations with members who are competent in computers will do well to enlist their help in introducing computers to the church's classroom.

The computer should not be looked upon as a new toy, the latest technique for holding the interest of a class. Film was used that way when it first became popular in churches, but, like any novelty, the excitement wore off. How film (or videotape) became integrated as part of a method determined its educational usefulness. So it must be for the computer. If a task can be as easily and less expensively accomplished by traditional ways of storytelling, discussion, drill, or games, it makes no sense to buy a computer. Yet its widespread use in schools to assist learning suggests that churches and their denominational education departments need to consider seriously how it can enrich Bible study.

Computers are also used in desktop publishing. Many church bulletins now look like printed programs. The parish publication takes on the appearance of a periodical. Yet print alone does not make it attractive. The skill of the compiler is essential. Still, appearance encourages creativity. In addition, teaching materials can now be done in the parish and be attractive enough to engage the interest of learners. Nationally sold curricular materials, whether denominational or independent, are currently facing challenges from parish-produced materials, where volume is not necessary and specific local needs can be met. A course of study can be written for city, rural, or suburban settings, for ethnic groups, for the competence of a specific age level.

---

15. See E. V. Clements, *Using Computers in Religious Education* (Nashville: Abingdon, 1986), for a practical manual.

A closer identity can be made between the biblical material and the illustrations used. Materials and methods locally available can be written into the directions. Churches that have been developing their own units of study have found a cohesiveness among teachers, families, and learners, and a high level of involvement, that has brought a new dynamic to the year's study. It is a trend that can only increase.

THE USES OF VIDEO

The use of television has been assumed under several other methods. Biblical films are viewed on videotape. The videotape of an oratorio or other biblical choral music can be used either for teaching or for a worship service.

Courses for biblical study are also available on videotape. This might be a series, with a distinguished biblical scholar as lecturer. The lecture (or even part of it) would be the basis for discussion in a class. It could be used as an introduction to biblical study, or preliminary study could prepare the class for this advanced presentation. The teacher's skill lies in knowing how to make the lecture enriching for the class.

Another type of videotape presents a discussion by a panel. An appropriate topic for a Bible study class might focus on an underlying assumption, such as the meaning of revelation or biblical authority. The class discussion is then deepened by these insights. (The class might have begun with discussion as a way to prepare for the panel.) Another video format might center on the responses of a number of people, lay and clergy, to the question, What does the Bible mean to me? or How is God present in my life?

Do not neglect the possibility of putting biblical programs on your local station. One theological seminary, for instance, broadcasts lectures of interest to the whole community. Such programming has the advantage of being available to families at home.

THE INTELLECTUAL TASK:
REASONING ABOUT THE BIBLE

The discussion so far has focused on methods for personal understanding of the Bible. Such understanding is incomplete until a person is able to share it with others. One approach is with intent to persuade others to become Christian. This is evangelism. When faith in Christ is integral to a person's life, the eagerness to share becomes a factor in telling the story. Another approach seeks to share what Christians believe with those of another faith, or none at all, who want to understand the Christian faith. This is the path to interfaith understanding and requires that Christians know something about other approaches to God in order to phrase their explanation in ways that a stranger would understand.

The writer of 1 Peter says when Christians are misunderstood and suffer on this account, they should "always be ready to make your defense to anyone who demands from you an accounting for the hope that is in you" (3:15). The New International Version keeps the usage of the Authorized Version: "Always be prepared to give an answer to everyone who asks you to give the reason for the hope that you have." This invites us to think about the meaning of our faith, for the frequent question is, Why do you believe? or How can you believe this? Catholics with traditional education used to be able to give answers, even when they were less certain about how to discuss their answers. Protestants have been known as people who could see many possible answers but few certainties. In order to discuss the Christian understanding of God, which to Jews and Muslims hardly seems to be the worship of one God, Christians need to have thought deeply about their allegiance to Christ in relation to their worship of God. There were centuries when Muslim and Christian scholars conversed. Jesuit and Confucian scholars shared their knowledge at the Chinese court.

Today many predominantly Christian nations have large populations who confess other religions. Christians need to be able to converse with them. Young people's groups visit not only churches of other Christian denominations or synagogues. They may visit the local mosque or Buddhist temple. The necessity for explaining one's own faith can bring clarity and lead to the ability to articulate it.

However high the percentage of people who affirm themselves to be Christian, there are many unchurched people. Some are disaffected; others grew up in a nonreligious family. Christians need to be able to speak to people whose only knowledge comes from the media, who see no need for religion in their lives but who are good people, loving and concerned. What does faith have to offer that they do not already have?

It is only through a deep grounding in the biblical faith that believers can enter into discussion with others. The Scriptures define and describe us, as those of other faiths are defined by their Scriptures, and nonbelievers are defined by their philosophies of life.

The church has largely neglected this approach to education. Even in Confirmation classes, where people are affirming their faith as adult

Christians, the emphasis is on learning content. Secondary education is supposed to challenge adolescents to think and to explore ideas. By the age of eleven or twelve they are beginning to ask questions about God and to question stories they have been told from the Bible. Frequently they do not raise these questions in church settings. Either they do not want to shock their pastor and teachers, whom they respect, or they expect to be rebuked for questioning sacred texts. Teachers need the gifts of conviction and openness. Commitment makes it possible for a person to explore options and to realize that a growing faith is one that can be enriched and deepened by new insights.

Adults as well as young people need to be engaged in the task of verbalizing their faith. This calls for discussion methods that probe beneath the surface when raising questions that have more than one answer. Sometimes people need to be unsettled in their thinking before they can become settled on a firmer foundation. Use debates, panel discussions, and symposiums to become exposed to different view-points. Use role-playing to practice presenting biblical understandings to those who question either from lack of knowledge or from rejection. Learn how to give a reason for the faith that is in you.

LEARNING ABOUT CHRISTIAN LIVING THROUGH THE BIBLE

Learning by doing has become a catchword in education. Learning vicariously through participation in story, music, or visual expressions is important. Learning through creative and constructive activities has its value. Expressing the meaning of the biblical message through deeds affirms that the understanding of Scripture must be seen in changed lives. To become involved in the story of the Bible is to live as it teaches. This always presents difficulties because of the need to translate a distant geographical, historical, and sociological situation into contemporary terms. A discussion of the meaning of the Bible in Christian living will be found in chapter 10. The practical aspects are outlined here. Methods for doing this can be as simple as the visit of a preschool class to a nursing home to sing Christmas carols. It can mean collecting toys for children in a hospital. Older children run errands for housebound neighbors. A Confirmation class may have as an assignment fulfilling a specified number of hours in community service. Adolescents become active in protest marches and silent vigils, as do their elders.

Parishes may neglect to lift up to their own view the ways in which members are living the gospel. Some work is done with deliberate intent as a congregation: money given for projects, work accomplished by groups. Vastly more outreach comes from individuals in personally chosen community activities at food centers, hospitals, in tutoring and giving personal support. All members need to know about such activities. Outreach activities structured into parish life obviously carry the stamp of being Christian witness. The everyday living of the gospel by individuals is done in this spirit, but without visible labeling. The cup of cold water given to the thirsty is still offered in Christ's name, but the intention resides in the compassion of the giver, without verbal attribution.

In the Jewish tradition, this keeping of Torah is called *Mitzvoth,* good deeds. From the early church comes the word *caritas,* deeds of loving-kindness. The English cognate, *charity,* has sometimes been interpreted to suggest a gift given to demonstrate superiority to people who cannot reciprocate. This is a mistake. Paul speaks of *caritas* as greater than faith or hope.

Living the gospel will be reflected in family, community, and church relationships. People need help in understanding how this can be accomplished, human nature being so far from perfect. Reflection on biblical stories and passages, and the sharing of personal experiences, can be mutually supportive.

Children and
the Bible

CHILDREN AND THE BIBLE SEEM TO GO TOGETHER in any discussion of religious education. Indeed, the biblical knowledge of many people is confined to children's Bible stories and Scripture reading in the Sunday service. This being the situation, the introduction of the Bible to children should leave them knowing the basic story, give them a ground for further interpretation, and encourage them to see themselves and God's action in the sacred texts.

UNDERSTANDING CHILDREN

The work of two psychologists has been highly influential in children's education in recent decades, and each has some implications for religious education.

Erik Erikson's theories revolve around psychosocial development. He was concerned to discover how children grow as persons within their social setting. The infant, he affirmed, requires a nurturing situation, where people who care give warmth and affection and meet basic needs, so that the child can believe that the world is to be trusted. The opposite is an uncertainty that leads to basic mistrust. Erikson adds that those who want children to grow up with religious faith need to realize that basic trust is the foundation for faith.

Two- and three-year-olds are developing autonomy. They want to make decisions, to say yes or no. They want freedom, but they also want the security of boundaries. Pressured too far for obedience, they will develop a sense of shame and doubt. Four- and five-year-olds are developing initiative, a continued exploration of the sense of self. They

begin to identify with the people closest to them. They need opportunities through their activities to explore varieties of roles. They are
developing a sense of right and wrong (conscience) as the internalized
voice of the parent.

By the age of six the emotional tasks for social development have
been met in one way or another. The six-year-old, entering the elementary school years, should have a sense of basic trust in people,
some degree of autonomy, and some capacity for showing initiative.
The various social and emotional settings in which the child has lived,
however, may have thwarted development instead of nurturing it. For
during the years from six to twelve the basic task is to learn the skills
needed for life in society. Erikson refers to it as the stage of industry.
Children enjoy concrete learning and are stimulated by their own
success. Those who struggle without accomplishing a task, on the
contrary, develop a sense of inferiority that could influence them
for life.

Jean Piaget, a Swiss psychologist, was concerned with cognitive
development. Carefully watching children from birth on, he evolved
his developmental stage theory. The child from birth to two is in a
sensori-motor stage, exploring and manipulating the immediate environment. Children from two to seven are in a pre-operational stage.
They are exploring the human environment and relationships
to people.

Children of elementary school age are in the concrete operational
stage. Cognitive learning expands as they are given experiences
through which they can explore their environment. Learning takes
place at each of these stages because the child accommodates the self
to the new learning and assimilates it, incorporating it and using it.
This is the process of adaptation.

Abstract operational learning begins to develop at the age of ten or
eleven. This is the ability to think conceptually, to form and discuss
ideas. Concrete operational learning is important because this is the
basis on which conceptual and abstract learning can take place.

The theories of Erikson and Piaget are supplemental. Both are
important for biblical teaching and learning. The Bible contains basic
content for Christian faith. Interpreting the Bible is important to
understanding.

Sensitivity to these developmental stages prompts teachers and parents to choose biblical material carefully. Verses of assurance that God
can be trusted will be used early. "God cares about you," "When I am
afraid, I will put my trust in you." The Psalms have many such verses,
as have the Gospels.

Biblical stories told to preschoolers will be chosen with an awareness of this development. They do not need to be stories about children. These are few and invariably concern children in threatening situations: Moses, Samuel, and even the baby Jesus. Doubtless these will continue to be used. Teachers will continue to point to God's care and the concern of parents, but they need also to be aware that for some of the listening children, the threat of separation, either physical or psychological, is real. How then will these stories be approached? How can the child affirm trust in God when adults cannot be trusted? Those who tell Bible stories need to know how the hearers will interpret them. Other stories tell of God's care and of ways in which people developed autonomy before God. Jacob is away from home and fearful but is given the assurance of God's presence. Jesus calls the children to him and takes them in his arms. Abraham is willing to go to a strange place. Four fishermen decide to answer the call to go with Jesus.

Children will also be given an opportunity to play out the stories, not as individuals taking roles, but as a group putting themselves in a biblical setting. Playing with nativity figures and other biblical figures will give them a tangible relationship to the stories.

Both Erikson's stage of industry and Piaget's concrete operational stage coincide in the elementary years (six–eleven). These are the years in which young Christians will learn the story, not simply disconnected stories. They do not need to have advanced cognitively to the stage where they can understand historical time in order to learn the story in chronological order. The younger children need stories about people with whom they can identify. Recognizing God's presence in those lives assures children that God is active in their own lives. Older children can hear the sequence from creation through the Gospels.

Several decades ago an English educator, Ronald Goldman, applied Piaget's categories to religious understanding, telling a selected group of children ages five to fourteen several Bible stories and asking questions to ascertain the children's understanding of the content. Responding to the story of the burning bush and that of the temptation of Jesus, the younger children interpreted these literally. After the age of eleven they began to become aware of symbolism or of spiritual meanings. His conclusion was that children should not have to deal with many Bible stories at an early age.[1] This conclusion has long affected curriculum building and there has been a concern to use biblical material that was both concrete and clear in meaning.

---

1. Ronald Goldman, *Religious Thinking from Childhood to Adolescence* (London: Routledge & Kegan Paul, 1964).

Now the pendulum has swung the other way. David Elkind, also an interpreter of Piaget, draws differing conclusions.[2] The processes of adaptation ensure that the child will grow from a simple understanding of religious phenomena to a fuller understanding through the reality of growing from concrete to abstract operational thinking. Children need to participate in the religious observances of their elders in order to absorb and participate in their faith. This is one way of learning. By implication, the telling of biblical stories, "our story," by the elders—parents, teachers, pastors—helps them to understand how they belong to the Christian community.

Another dimension is brought to the discussion by an emphasis on the spiritual aspect of life. According to James M. Fowler's theory of faith development, having faith is inborn and matures by stages through our relationships to others.[3] Preschool children have an intuitive faith, they "feel" it. The second stage is the "mythic-literal," that of the school-age child. It is concrete. This suggests that preschool children can identify with the feelings expressed in specifically chosen biblical materials. Elementary children will hear the stories concretely. In later childhood, the synthetic-conventional stage, they will accept the tradition with which they are surrounded in home and church. So the sharing of biblical stories and passages becomes part of incorporation into the community of faith.

Edward Robinson, from the Religious Experience Research Unit of Manchester College, England, goes in a direction different from the developmentalists.[4] He asked older people to recall spiritual experiences from their childhood. Their remembrances were of deep awareness of the transcendent, of a sense of God known through people and the world. But, interestingly, although they were asked to recall experiences with family, in church, or in school (religious education classes), the respondents made little reference to the Bible. Even in answer to a question about the sources of their understanding of God, they referred to family. This is significant in a negative way. It indicates the possibility that Bible stories heard in school and at worship do not necessarily connect with an understanding of God, prayer, strength

---

2. David Elkind, *The Child's Reality: Three Developmental Themes* (Hillsdale, N.J.: Lawrence Erlbaum Associates, 1978), part i, "Religious Development," pp. 1-45.

3. James W. Fowler, *Stages of Faith: The Psychology of Human Development and the Quest for Meaning* (San Francisco: Harper & Row, 1981).

4. *The Original Vision: A Study of the Religious Experience of Childhood* (New York: Seabury Press, 1983). Sofia Cavalletti makes similar observations from her conversations with young children (see footnote 13).

for living, or anything else that we hope will come from biblical teaching.

Across several decades Robert Coles has been gathering significant insights into the lives of children through sensitively phrased questions that encourage self-revelation. In his book *The Spiritual Life of Children,* their interpretative drawings of Bible stories indicate clear personal meaning.

He writes,

> Biblical stories . . . have a way of being used by children to look inward as well as upward. It should come as no surprise that the stories of Adam and Eve, Abraham and Isaac, Noah and the Ark, Abel and Cain, Samson and Delilah, David and Goliath, get linked in the minds of millions of children to their own personal stories as they explore the nature of sexuality and regard with awe, envy, or anger the power of their parents, as they wonder how solid and lasting their world is, as they struggle with brothers and sisters, as they imagine themselves as actual or potential lovers, or as actual or potential antagonists. The stories are not mere symbolism, giving expression to what people go through emotionally. Rather, I hear children embracing religious stories because they are quite literally inspiring—exciting their minds to further thought and fantasy and helping them become more grown, more contemplative and sure of themselves.[5]

The story of David and Goliath gives strength to Timmy in his growing.[6] Josephine, explaining her drawing of Jesus healing a leper, says that there are people today treated like lepers, and if we are following Jesus we should be trying to help them.[7] Later Coles notes, "For many Christian children Jesus becomes not so much a revered, inspirational figure, nor God's Son, hence powerful and knowing beyond measure, but a children's Savior: the One who survived childhood and later suffering, and is still very much present."[8]

This background to children's religious development can be helpful for exploring ways to teach the Bible to children.

---

5. *The Spiritual Life of Children* (Boston: Houghton Mifflin, 1990), p. 121.
6. Ibid., p. 126.
7. Ibid., pp. 173-75.
8. Ibid. p. 209.

Cole's observations, and some of the stories he uses illustratively, speak to the question of biblical violence and children. Violence in the neighborhood and around the world comes into view for children through television, film, the daily news, and tragically through everyday experience. The violence described in the Bible pales into insignificance. To begin with, it is understated. There are no gory details for the imagination. Moreover usually the good person triumphs: Joseph, Moses, David, Elijah, Daniel. The story of Cain and Abel, however, is ugly and is usually withheld from younger children. When heard, it needs to be dealt with as the tragedy it represents. Remember that God condemned Cain's act but protected him from revenge. Sibling rivalry—Jacob and Esau, Joseph and his brothers—is something children understand and can identify with, although it is not usually played out to such drastic ends. The disciples quarreling over who would be first in the kingdom represent a situation that children know.

The historical books are replete with wars hardly different from those that older children learn about in school. The problem arises when—because the Bible is theologically oriented—such wars are described as either commanded by God or waged in disobedience. In either case, the judgment is divine. The interpretation indicates how the result was the outcome of actions, and not a vengeful act of God. Remember that Isaiah and Jeremiah promised restoration.

The crucifixion is known to children at an early age, and keeping it from the printed material serves no purpose. Palm Sunday is not a joyous event but the foreshadowing of the coming Friday. Without the cross there is no resurrection. This is the reason for linking the two events for children. The freely given self-offering of Jesus fulfilled his special calling, and God was with him, as Easter Sunday proclaims.

The concern about teaching children biblical stories that include violence may have more to do with the sensitivities of adults than with those of children. The latter are realists. The gospel is good news, always—the good news of God's redeeming love.

APPROACHING THE BIBLE WITH CHILDREN

Methods for teaching are the way by which children are brought to the Bible story. You have just read a whole chapter on methods. Methods are not just chosen at random and strung together to fill the time allotted to a teaching session. Methods derive from a methodology: the plan in back of the methods teachers choose. The goal needs to be appropriate to the age and experiences of the learners and must effectively convey the meaning of the Bible.

Dorothy Jean Furnish, working with teachers and children across a number of years, has developed such a methodology. She states, "The goal of Bible study with children is to help them deal with the 'meaning' questions of their lives as they discover meanings in the Bible."[9] She wants to avoid the supposed dichotomy between teaching that is biblically oriented and teaching that arises from the life experience of learners. She adds, "When children experience the Bible, they discover meaning in their own experiences because the Bible deals with human concerns. It speaks to the reality within each child, thus becoming a 'now' event."[10]

Her methodology is outlined in her book *Living the Bible with Children*.[11] The first step is to "feel into" the text, whether it is a verse, a passage, or a story. Methods chosen will enable the children to identify with the biblical people in order to become involved in the story. It is not a matter of following a chronology of events or understanding the meaning of words. This would be a cognitive approach, which has its own value but does not make the Bible a living word to Christian learners today.

The next step is to "meet with" the text so that it confronts them. God continues to speak through these people. Seeing ourselves in the text makes it possible to meet with God. The third step is to "respond out of" the text. What is the Bible calling the hearer to do? This could be an immediate personal response such as drawing a picture or writing a poem. It could be an act of service by individuals or the group.

If a class was being introduced to the story of the reunion of Joseph with his brothers (Genesis 44-45), the teacher might begin by asking them to share a time when a wrong had been done to them. How did they feel? What did they do? Recall the way in which Joseph had been treated by his brothers. Then tell the story of their visit to Egypt to obtain food and the revelation of Joseph as their brother. "Acting out of the story" involves finding identifications. Did you feel like Joseph? Would you have acted as he did? Did you feel like any of the brothers? Was he wrong to have put them in such a perilous situation? How did the story turn out? Do you like this ending? Give the children opportunity to draw or paint whatever response they wish in biblical terms or from their own experience.

---

9. *Exploring the Bible with Children* (Nashville: Abingdon, 1975), p. 15.

10. Ibid., p. 99.

11. (Nashville: Abingdon, 1979), sect. 2, pp. 36-85.

You can see how the purpose of Bible teaching in a particular context determines both the methodology and the flow of the methods chosen.

Jerome Berryman has a creative methodology—and methods—that he describes under the evocative title *Godly Play*. He believes that "children need to learn how to wonder in religious education so they can 'enter' religious language rather than merely repeat it or talk about it. They need to be able to work together, to choose their own work—and return to it whenever they wish." He sees the need for children to learn "the art of using religious language" and to have an environment that supports this. He wants religious education to be shaped by the structure of the Eucharist. He adds, "The child's encounter with God can be achieved only indirectly. Even if the six objectives are taken care of by the teaching team, the child's encounter with God is a relationship that is beyond the team's control."[12]

Berryman's methods grow out of the work of Maria Montessori through Sofia Cavalletti.[13] It is a clear departure from the usual classroom. Drawing also on the work of biblical scholar John Dominic Crossan, whose work was referred to here in chapter 2, he thinks it important to vicariously place the children in a biblical setting.

Under the heading of the unspoken lesson, he describes a teaching space where all the materials are on shelves. The central altar shelf contains the materials of Easter, Christmas, Baptism, and Eucharist. The storyteller sits in front of this place. On the sides are gold boxes with parable materials, other Gospel stories, and Old Testament stories. The materials consist of a felt setting to be rolled into place and figures to be placed on it.[14] After each arriving child has been greeted and has found a place in the circle, the presenter takes materials from the shelf, unrolls the setting, and tells the story. The children are involved in placing objects. In the quiet after the children's comments, each selects materials for drawing a response. Later they return to the circle to find a cloth spread on which juice and simple food has been placed. Each prays, aloud or silently (or passes up the invitation). They eat and then are dismissed, one at a time. It is a quiet, deliberate pace.[15]

Godly play "contrasts talking *about* Scripture and worship with being *in* scripture and worship."[16] This is an imaginative approach.

---

12. Jerome W. Berryman, *Godly Play: A Way of Religious Education* (San Francisco: Harper San Francisco, 1991), p. 60.

13. *The Religious Potential of the Child: The Description of an Experience with Children from Ages Three to Six* (Ramsey: Paulist Press, 1983).

14. *Godly Play*, pp. 19–22.

15. Ibid., pp. 28–41.

16. Ibid., p. 68. Berryman describes how a series of pictures drawn by each of two boys during a twelve-week period illustrated the way in which a parable (the mustard seed) came to grow in meaning for the children (pp. 44–59).

The Bible story is basic, told within the liturgical context (including the church year), but it leads the children to see its relationship to their own lives.

These are suggested approaches for helping children know the Bible. They do not give criteria for selecting Bible stories. Remember that the Bible tells about basic human experiences that affect children as much as adults. It is important to be faithful to the intent of the story and not to distort its meaning in order to make a particular story comprehensible to children. Some stories should not be used for pre-schoolers. Instead of oversimplifying, recognize that they will be able to identify with the story better when they are eight years old. We are particularly prone to oversimplification when we interpret parables. This is where Berryman's approach is instructive. Parables were meant to be self-interpreting in surprising ways, as Crossan points out, and this is exactly what the method of playing with parables does. The feeding of the multitude is often distorted by using the version in John's Gospel and putting the emphasis on the boy who shared his lunch. Bringing him in as someone the children cam identify with is all right, but putting the emphasis on him distorts the narrative. The focus of the Gospel story is on Jesus, his act of feeding, and the reaction of those who participated. It is therefore more as participants than as givers that hearers come to the story, as did the boy.

Most important, as these teachers have indicated, biblical stories do not need to be interpreted by teachers. They need to be assimilated by hearers, who then do their own interpreting in words or graphics. They may be willing to share these insights, but they will surely have to sense the meaning for themselves.

READING AND UNDERSTANDING THE STORY

Children are learning skills at school that challenge them to think, skills barely touched in religious education classes. Beginning in first grade, children have a growing facility in reading, encouraged by special reading programs and incentives in school. They are taught to read for comprehension and interpretation. Reading aloud to the class is only one approach and is used with the younger children as they are putting sound and sight together and expressing meaning through speech.

When cognition is an aspect of learning, there are ways of making this a lively part of the session. The traditional way of reading around a circle is deadly! It causes embarrassment to slow readers, who must struggle publicly. Fast readers are bored. Interested readers have finished pages before the class has completed a few paragraphs. Practicing the skill of reading is not a responsibility of the religious education class. Using the skill is.

The teacher should write on the chalkboard a reference to specific biblical verses or a section from the classbook and questions to be thought about during the silent reading. When all have completed the reading, the questions can be answered and discussed. This gives the teacher an opportunity to ascertain whether all have read the essential facts. Then the children will be prepared to discuss the meaning of the reading.

Upper elementary children, still willing to hear Bible stories told, are ready to read the text for themselves. You will want to choose a translation carefully, and several new ones are attractively arranged. The American Bible Society has large-print editions of the New Testament, individual books and stories, and illustrated editions to make Bible reading inviting.[17]

In biblical study it is important first to see the text in its own setting. This is why we help children try to understand nomadic cultures, ancient villages, or a Roman city. The text is placed within the setting so that the references may be clear. Shepherding in Montana is not the same as in the Holy Land two thousand years ago, but the sense of security children feel hearing a story of the shepherd's care has meaning to children in any place. Then readers need to hear how the text was understood by those to whom it was first spoken. Finally they need to hear it spoken to their situation, the point at which the Bible becomes contemporary.

Older children have skills from school to help them in biblical research. They know how to use maps and atlases. They understand word study and could be introduced to a children's Bible dictionary and encyclopedia. They also need maps of biblical lands, charts, and time lines. Even younger children can use vocabulary study. Because biblical words—the entire language of faith—is beyond the secular school curriculum, unless we teach it children will never learn it.

A chronological approach to the Bible is also important. Unless this is part of the curriculum process, children will grow up not knowing where to place Sarah in relation to Mary or David in relation to John. This ignorance is often cited in surveys lamenting the biblical ignorance of teenagers. The way to avoid this is consistently to arrange

---

17. The American Bible Society, 1865 Broadway, New York, NY 10023.

materials in chronological order. Books used by early elementary children should have biblical stories arranged from Genesis through Acts. This goes against the grain of topical teaching, where stories are arranged under headings such as "Families," "Helpers," and "Great Leaders." Older elementary children, developing a sense of history, need to learn the whole story of the Bible over a two-year period.

The messages of the prophets would be included in this approach. The Psalms would be used to illustrate different concerns and to recapitulate the history, as in Psalm 136. Brief quotations from Paul's letters would illumine the story of the apostolic church.

Children are aware of what is going on in the world: conflict, poverty, injustice. Passages from the Prophets and the Gospels will give them a basis for exploring their concerns and questions. Illustrating biblical passages with pictures from newspapers and newsmagazines will bring out the contemporaneity of the words. Reflections on television programs present an opportunity for relating this daily experience to biblical learning.

Older children are beginning to think conceptually. They may find dissonance between information from school subjects, in literature as well as science, and what they hear on Sunday. The approaches suggested so far have seemed to bypass this possible conflict by leading children to an inner apprehension of the biblical text or story. What of the child who asks, "Is this true?" This is a question about "fact" versus "truth," which was discussed in chapter 3. Older children need opportunities to explore the question freely, assured of the acceptance and understanding of adults. Encourage them to compare the several ways in which a story is told in the Bible. This may be found in books of Gospel parallels, which follow each Gospel's narrative and show the other Gospels' counterparts in parallel columns. Talk about the meaning conveyed by each version, and note the emphasis of the particular setting for each passage. Through such searching, learners will begin to develop a personal faith. It is important that they be able to do this within the church community and to realize that others at their age are also probing biblical meanings. Teachers need to clarify their own theological and biblical understandings in order both to accept and to guide young learners with their questions.

This is a time for being honest about biblical people. They are human, like the rest of us. Selected stories may be fine for younger children, but older children need to hear the whole story. This is the good news! The people in the Bible were chosen by God, courageous and dedicated—and sinful. They are believable only when seen as fully human. So the whole story needs to be read or told. Our problem, as teachers, comes with interpretation. The Bible is austerely dramatic in its storytelling. Teachers who try to elaborate, either to make a story more vivid or to tone down unpleasant aspects, lose the power of the original narrative.

Psalms are taught from the earliest years. Verses of joy and thanksgiving help preschool children express their love of God through worship and as a response to story. Shorter psalms and passages from psalms verbalize the needs of elementary children in joy, anger, disappointment, or praise. Psalms are a way of helping older children recapitulate the biblical story, to express the wonder of creation, to envision festivals and processions in ancient liturgy, and to affirm God's presence in their lives.

Biblical chronology has been suggested as a basic organizing center for teaching, but an alternative is the church year. The children follow the Gospel story from Advent to Pentecost. The other half of the church year, "ordinary time," can be devoted to the story of the early church and the Old Testament story. Several publishers are using the lectionary as the organizing principle. It is a more limited approach because it ties everyone to the same biblical material and requires the kind of adaptation to younger age levels that leads to the possibility of distortion. Following the church year does not necessarily mean using the lectionary but only following the Advent-to-Pentecost sequence, using Gospel materials fitted to specific age levels.

EXPRESSING THE CHILD'S UNDERSTANDING
OF THE BIBLE

So far we have been concerned with verbal material: the Bible story in the text or an adaptation. This story has inspired expression in many mediums.

Great artists have a profound understanding of the Bible. This is their gift. The simplicity of a Rembrandt print or the fantasy quality of a Chagall Bible illustration will give children an interpretation to arouse their own imagination and creativity. Photographs of the biblical lands and people and of ancient ruins help to interpret the meaning of the Bible. (This is discussed in chapter 4, but teachers of children frequently believe that only the illustrations that come with curriculum materials can be understood by children.) When you take children to a museum, see what pictures or artifacts from ancient civilizations appeal to them. Museums usually have docents who work only with children and know exactly how to involve them in the art.

Music does not need to be confined to what is found in a children's hymnal. Children learn complicated Christmas carols at any early age. The refrains from many church hymns can be used with preschool children. The melodies of many hymns, old and new, can be easily learned by elementary-age children. Perhaps one particular stanza suits your study. Look up psalms such as "All People That on Earth Do Dwell." Hymns about the ministry of Jesus, the passion, and Easter are moving commentaries on the story. With older children, use the words of hymns to explore further meanings. For example, note Passover references in Easter hymns. The simplicity of folk tunes, spirituals, and contemporary hymns is appealing.

Enrichments for teaching are important. Classrooms should have materials equivalent to those the child would find at school during the week. There should be extra books that children can pick up for themselves or ask teachers and parents to read to them. Books with cassettes are not a substitute for storytelling, but they offer a way of reading to the child who wants to be alone. Older children need well-written stories of biblical people and events. Many children are encouraged by their schools and families to enjoy reading. Too little is available that can help them grow into their biblical heritage. It would also be helpful to have a lending library of children's Bible books to be used at home. Make a selected list of such books and give them to parents to encourage them to buy Bible storybooks.

Children need also to be able to express their own learning. Teachers will never know what a particular biblical story or passage means to a child until this opportunity is given. Some children will simply draw what they think they see (especially when given an illustration). Others will interpret the story in terms of their experience. Writing is another form of interpretation. Some prefer to write by way of cassette, speaking their story on tape. Some can express themselves in poetry. One value of the learning center approach is that it offers children a variety of materials with which to express their learning. Informal dramatization brings out interpretation when the children see their own life mirrored in the biblical story. Think about the family tensions between Jacob and Esau![18]

To some extent methods of teaching need to be age-graded, but there is a wide area of adaptation, and children overlap age boundaries

---

18. Helpful ways of teaching children will be found in A. Roger Gobbel and Gertrude G. Gobbel, *The Bible: A Child's Playground* (Philadelphia: Fortress Press, 1986); and Patricia Van Ness, *Transforming Bible Study with Children* (Nashville: Abingdon, 1991).

in their ways of expression. Just as a well-told story can be absorbing to children and adults, other approaches can appeal equally to a wide age range. As all adult members of families know, you can read some books innumerable times to a five-year-old, while other books leave them bored after the first reading. Stories need to be vivid and involve the listener.

The Bible is for reading, enjoying, and repeating.

Young People
and the Bible

YOUNG PEOPLE ARE A CHALLENGE to the church because the potential for serious Bible study exists but the knowledge they bring to such study is minimal. They remember Bible stories from childhood, complete with their childhood interpretations. If they are not enabled to see the Bible from a more mature perspective, however, they may assume that it will not speak to them in adulthood.

UNDERSTANDING THEIR NEEDS AS GROWING PERSONS

For several decades now, adolescent development has been understood as a time for forming self-identity (versus identity diffusion), based on the psychosocial stages set forth by Erik Erikson. According to Erikson, although one stage takes precedence over the rest at a particular age level, the need to establish self-identity persists in some form throughout life. In achieving this task of self-identity, the young person needs continuing relationships with adults that ensure the trustworthiness of people and the world, increasing opportunity for making serious choices so that autonomy continues to develop, broader freedom to establish responsibility, and sufficient success in learning to feel accomplished.

Self-identity is the task of the adolescent, and the quest to achieve this motivates (usually unconsciously) attitudes and actions. A number of factors are involved. Physical development, including sexual maturing, is one process, and it deeply affects relationships with peers. The relationship with family changes as the adolescent strives toward autonomy and the elders balance that need with the desire to set protective boundaries. Balancing school and family values with their own needs and desires compels them to face the question, "What kind of person am I?" Similarly interaction with peers and the community brings up questions of responsibility toward others. Achieving good grades, successfully completing the course, is also an overarching need. This is the key to acceptance into the adult world, whether it is work or further education.

At this point, Jean Piaget's cognitive stage theory enters in. Adolescents are capable of formal operations, or abstract operational thinking. They can probe facts in order to question information, deepen learning, or think through issues. In terms of James M. Fowler's faith development stages, young people are at a synthetic-conventional faith; that is, they are comfortable in the faith in which they find themselves. Older young people are beginning to experience an individuative-reflective faith growing out of increasing autonomy.

Adolescence has been called a bridge or transitional stage. It may seem so, because the young person is leaving childhood and striving to be considered an adult. But the importance of the task makes it a stage with its own integrity. The length of time spent in this stage may vary according to the person, family, and culture, but it exists.[1]

In the mid-1980s the Lilly Foundation funded a Youth Ministry in Theological Schools project that resulted in a number of studies and books.[2] Assessing the situation of adolescents, the study affirmed that some subcultures were withdrawing from the church, and ways of understanding their needs was essential. Many suffered from low self-esteem. The suicide rate was high. Many adolescents had experienced drug dependency, family estrangement, and abuse. In a climate of ethical relativity and a loss of the notion of truth, they searched for moral stability. They lacked boundaries for sexual behavior. (This was highlighted in the spring of 1993 by widespread allegations of rape in a suburban Los Angeles high school.) They had questions about homosexuality. They were searching for meaning and a sense of vocation.

Ethnic identity was strong in some minority groups. This is outlined in a book that grew out of the Lilly studies, *Black and White: Styles of*

---

1. Perceptive books delineating the situation of adolescents are Peter Benson, Dorothy Williams, and Arthur Johnson, *The Quicksilver Years: The Hopes and Fears of Early Adolescence* (San Francisco: Harper & Row, 1987), a study by the SEARCH Institute; and David Elkind, *All Grown Up and No Place to Go: Teenagers in Crisis* (Reading, Mass.: Addison-Wesley, 1984).

2. "Youth Ministry and Theological Education: An Agenda for Change," position statement of the Chicago Lilly seminar (Youth Ministry and Theological Schools Project, June 30, 1988, project director Sara Little).

Youth Ministry. Comparing the teaching agendas of two large Chicago-area churches, the author discovered that young people in the white church learned to be middle class, morally good, competent managers, friendly, and to avoid being different from their group. Young people in the black church learned to be unashamedly black, unapologetically Christian, competent adults, politically aware, and developing a lifestyle.[3]

John and Catherine Nelson of the Center for Youth Ministry as part of a research project called "The Adolescent Quest for Meaning" use the word *mindset* to describe one of the dimensions of being human and apply this to adolescent development. A mindset combines "how we image our world and feel about it, how we organize it into categories, what judgments we make about its truth, what decisions we make in terms of its value, how we behave day-to-day as a result of the way we sort out lives."[4] To them the relational identity of adolescence is important, and they list five present day factors significant in establishing personal identity to make relationships with other persons possible. The prolongation of adolescence provides a longer time for accomplishing developmental tasks. The feminist revolution has opened up understanding of gender likenesses and differences between young men and women (e.g. Carol Gilligan's work on gender differences). Relationship models are conveyed through the media, especially television and music. Computer literacy both brings people together and keeps them apart. Awareness of the inadequacy of the American emphasis on individualism is leading to thoughtful consideration of the need for commitment.[5]

IMPLICATIONS FOR BIBLE STUDY

No one claims that it is easy to interest young people in Bible study. Nor will there be any agreement on the continuing question as to whether to begin with the Bible or with life experience. One certainty is that those who are engaged in the quest with young people must themselves have mature understanding of the Bible and an awareness

---

3. By William R. Myers (New York: Pilgrim Press, 1991), pp. 170-71. See also by the same author, *Theological Themes of Youth Ministry* (New York: Pilgrim Press, 1987), for biblical bases in the church year.
4. *Mindsets for Adolescents: Religious and Otherwise,* Youth Ministry Resource Network, occasional paper no. 18 (Saugatuck, Conn.: Center for Youth Ministry Development, 1988), p. 3.
5. Ibid., pp. 7-9.

of its contemporaneity. Few people seem able to combine this with the gift of understanding young people and eliciting their confidence. Perhaps a team approach is needed.

The writers of *Helping Youth Interpret the Bible* are clear as to the task. "The period of adolescence," they write, "affords the church a unique opportunity to introduce, initiate, and aid teenagers in a larger task of interpreting the Bible than was possible for them as children. If we can but *introduce* and *initiate* our Christian youth into that larger work, we shall have served them well."[6]

Retelling Bible stories is not "mere" repetition, they assert, because young people will be hearing them from the context of their own wider perspective on life and their own ability to reason. In a survey of youth attitudes toward the Bible, the writers asked, "How important is it to read the Bible?" (answer: very). "Why do you think it is important to read the Bible?" (answer: it tells you how to behave, it helps you live a good life.) "How often do you read the Bible?" (answer: not very often; I can't understand it.)[7]

This response of church young people indicates that the biblical Word is not accessible to them, that it does not come to them in words or forms in which they can find meaning. It also says that their primary impression of the Bible is that of a rule book.[8]

Clearly there has been a misunderstanding. The stories from childhood did not convey the story. The invitation to study is not an open door but an impenetrable path. Young people have not looked at narrative as God's own self-disclosure, which is the way biblical scholars urge us to understand it. Young people need to uncover further dimensions in the Bible. If they still have unanswered questions from their childhood, they need to ask them again. If the difficult courses pursued each weekday in high school make Christian education class seem infantile, this needs to be corrected. Bible study includes the study of literature, history, sociology, geography, and theology.

Although a biblical passage read from the text may appear to young people quite different from the version they remember from a children's story, they may nevertheless be disturbed by the invitation to probe its meaning. Perhaps they have a lingering perception that questions are not to be asked of the Bible or that skepticism about its "truth" may not be admitted. If they think the Bible is important, but

---

6. By A. Roger Gobbel, Gertrude G. Gobbel, and Thomas E. Ridenhour, Sr. (Atlanta: John Knox Press, 1984), p. 3.

7. Ibid., p. 13.

8. This represented a group of young persons ages twelve to sixteen (ibid., p. 5).

have not found it so for their lives, this may cause discomfort when brought to the surface.

Many of these problems could have been avoided if as children these teenagers had been told Bible stories in a way that admitted and probed the conflicts in the lives of biblical people. A pattern of exploring the depths of those characters' experience encourages adolescent hearers to raise questions, to see contradictions, and to dispute conclusions. Unexamined faith is not strong. A vigorous encounter with the Bible can be an exhilarating experience. To begin with, the learner realizes that God is not threatened, either in being or activity. Sustained by believing and searching mentors—parents, teachers, pastors—young people discover that questioning does not destroy faith but rather gives a firmer foundation for a faith to match their stage in life.

It will be difficult for adults not to correct some of the responses of young people unless they have confidence that a willingness on the part of both to share doubts and convictions is a sign of trust and growth. This listening attitude is an assurance to young people that they are being taken seriously by adults in the church.

Effective leaders or teachers of youth gain their trust by being genuine and down to earth, according to Dick Murray.[9] Because most young people don't expect adults to tell the truth when teaching about the Bible, he says leaders need to counteract this impression by being honest about their own feelings, interpretations, and knowledge of the Bible (or lack thereof). Adolescents want a session that is relaxed and open, with time to laugh, but they also want some order. When they get out of line, this is not an attack on the teacher but a response to what is happening in their lives. Do not expect strokes, he advises. Their appreciation will be expressed sparsely and indirectly.

Thomas H. Groome provides a valuable methodology for teaching the Bible to adolescents.[10] It features five steps: present action (the whole self in the present context); critical reflection (through reason, memory, and imagination) to evaluate the present; dialogue within the setting (listening and telling); the story; and vision (the response).

Such a broadly stated methodology invites a variety of interpretations. Study might begin with a biblical passage, such as the dispute among the disciples over the request of James and John to be first in the kingdom (Matt. 20:20-28; Mark 10:35-45; Luke 22:24-27; and

---

9. *Teaching the Bible to Youth and Adults,* pp. 89-91.
10. *Christian Religious Education* (San Francisco: Harper San Francisco, 1980), chap. 9, pp. 184-95.

similarly in John 13:4-5, 12-17). The story begins with the request, gives the reaction of the disciples, and concludes with Jesus' admonition to all. In the reflective stage the questions to be asked are, Has anything like this ever happened to you? Where do you see yourself in this story? The incident could be dramatized at this point. This technique will bring out the feelings of the young people concerning those who want to be first. The topic of competition arises. The third movement is that of dialogue, where the biblical story and their stories are compared and all the responses of the group are heard.

The next step is biblical study (in contrast with the beginning, which was telling the story). Here the three versions are compared. The ironic allusion is noted (the two thieves were later at Jesus' left and right hand). The narrative from John, where Jesus, on the night of his betrayal, washes the disciples' feet as a sign of what it means to be a servant, is a commentary. As in the second movement, dialogue is the key to the method. Here the dialogue is with the Gospel writers in order to explore the nuances of meaning: What is present in one and omitted in another? The final step is vision. Essentially this is the question, What does this experience of the disciples with Jesus mean for each of us? The question could also be, What does this mean for our parish, the church, our family, community, nation?

The methodology might begin instead with experiences of the group or the recital of an incident where young people strove for precedence. The biblical story might then be the second step. This is meant not as a blueprint but as one suggestion for teachers exploring a passage with adolescents. Other methodologies will suggest themselves for particular goals in biblical study.

This approach achieves several important learning objectives. The biblical text is used, and different recitals of the story explored. The young people are introduced to exegesis. They view the passage in its setting. They are encouraged to make interpretations of the text and to find it validity for their lives.

In the study of longer texts, such as Mark's Gospel, you would want to have available tools for study: maps of the biblical world, a biblical dictionary, a one-volume commentary, and a concordance. You would also want to use several translations so that students can become aware of variations as scholars bring different purposes or viewpoints to the task.

FAITH AND KNOWLEDGE

The purpose of any approach to Bible study with adolescents is to permit them to use the critical intellectual faculties that are stretching their minds and exhilarating them through the questions they perceive. At the same time, it tries to help them make the transition from their childhood faith to the lifelong task of maturing as Christians, in the assurance that one can love God with both the mind and the affections and that one can know Jesus through the Gospels and serve him in all of life.

For many young people and their pastors, this task begins with the Confirmation or church membership class. It is useless to try to make this a wrap-up of years of religious education classes, even if experience tells you that they will never darken the doors of a Sunday school room again. By taking another approach, you can at least prepare them for hearing (not simply listening to) the Scripture readings during Sunday worship. To this end, it is important that they attend the Sunday service during the weeks that the class is being held. As a group they should read and reflect on one of the Bible passages used there.

Examine the outline for Sunday worship. Where is the Bible used? The Lord's Prayer has been called the prayer of the church because it was given by Jesus to the disciples. Try to "feel into" its meaning. Encourage the young people to use it thoughtfully in their own daily prayer.

Explore the liturgy your church uses for Confirmation. What are the biblical elements? Look up allusions and quotations, and probe their meaning.

You will also want to look at the baptismal liturgy (in those traditions that observe Baptism and Confirmation as separate events). Note biblical references to baptism in the Gospels and in the book of Acts. Some liturgies include Old Testament references. Consider these.

In some traditions Confirmation marks the admission of young people to the Lord's Supper. But those who have participated in the celebration of the Eucharist since an earlier age need the opportunity to reflect on it in a new way. What did it mean to them as children? Do they find other or different meanings now? What does it mean personally and as a member of the Christian community? Look at the liturgical text. Give attention to the words of institution. Look up the accounts in the Synoptic Gospels and in 1 Cor. 11:23-26. Talk about the text as theological reflection. In this study you are combining the meaning of the biblical text with the evocative power this act of worship has for Christians.

One is reminded of Anselm of Canterbury's words about faith seeking understanding. "I believe in order to understand," he wrote. He was saying that the Christian believes first, drawn by God's love to a response of devotion. In the same way, Martin Luther made a distinction between believing about and believing in. Faith is believing in, and this is the way the Creed is stated. We confess it; it is an act of worship. We also want to discuss its meaning, and there is a place for that. The Confirmation class in some traditions explores these dimensions of the historical creedal statements in their biblical settings.

Objective and subjective approaches have been described as the balcony view and the pilgrimage view of life, respectively. The academic study of the Bible seeks a more objective knowledge of the text and its meaning. The pilgrimage view studies the Bible from the viewpoint of a participant in the story, one who belongs in the succession of those whose lives were witnesses to faith in the living God. The two views are not mutually exclusive. Young people need to grow in the assurance that they can study, question, and doubt in order to grow in faith.

OCCASIONS FOR BIBLE STUDY

In his book *Teaching the Bible to Youth and Adults* Dick Murray affirms that "under the 'right' circumstances youth are 'turned on' to Bible study."[11] He suggests that there needs to be more flexible time slots and a variety of meeting places.

The traditional Protestant Sunday morning hour, preceding or following morning worship, may still work, especially in parishes where there are strong adult classes (frequently found in the South). In this context, going to Sunday school is something for adults, not just for children, and adolescents want to leave childhood activities behind and participate in adult activities. But it is difficult to generate or reinvigorate this pattern where it has not had a long-standing place. For adolescents, Saturday night is for fun and Sunday morning is for relaxing. If they attend worship (an adult activity), they are acting like adults. Evangelical churches are usually much more successful in maintaining Sunday school classes for adolescents than mainline churches are. Catholic parishes usually schedule educational events on weekdays.

The picture is complicated by the fact that school activities are frequently scheduled for Sunday. School and church no longer have a tacit agreement to reserve a specific time for religious education.

11. (Nashville: Abingdon, 1987), p. 86.

Church activities must be scheduled within the cracks left by school and extracurricular activities.

The good news is that Bible study is better done in small groups than in large groups, and this affords flexibility. Whatever overall programming is designed to give young people that necessary feeling of being part of a large group of their peers, there is still a place for forming small groups. These could meet at church or in homes. In some communities, youth groups gather after school in the school building. Small groups have the advantage of permitting a variety of formats. Young people might wish to study a book of the Bible, such as Galatians, or the biblical basis for a doctrine such as salvation. They might want to explore the understanding of justice in Micah or prayer in the Bible or to do a "Who am I?" study of Christian identity in biblical perspective."[12] When a group is formed, the members can agree as to the time, places, and number of sessions they wish to have, although modifications of these arrangements may be made as the study continues.

Sunday school and CCD teachers know that they learn by doing. Their own biblical understandings increase as they teach. High schoolers are excellent teacher's helpers because children enjoy them. They too can increase in biblical knowledge as they are given real responsibilities in storytelling and response to the story.

Church camps and conferences are valuable settings for Bible study because young people can take advantage of the concentrated time and the absence of everyday distractions. A unit of study designed within the camp or conference theme provides an opportunity for exploring the biblical text and responding in depth to its meaning for young people as individuals and in their lives in community.

Church young people are frequently involved in summer work camps. One California parish's high school group offered a vacation Bible school for the children on a Navaho reservation in a neighboring state. They were helped by the Navaho young people, who at a later time visited them in their suburban setting in California. Preparing, teaching, and reflecting after the event provided the opportunity for serious Bible exploration.

Reflection is an important word here. Doing requires preparation and the sharing of knowledge and experience. But reflecting afterward

---

12. A series of eight units "engaging and interpreting the Bible" from the perspective of teenagers' questions is carefully developed in Gobbel et al., *Helping Youth Interpret the Bible,* part 2, "Doing the Task," chaps. 6-11, pp. 75-202.

reveals how well the teachers are able to share and where they feel a need to increase their own knowledge and understanding.

Many high schools today give credit for community service, and Confirmation classes include this element as part of their preparation. Young people are aware of the deep problems of poverty and its attendant miseries of hunger and homelessness. Churches are deeply involved in the work of alleviating these needs, and community agencies welcome help from teenagers. This ministry grows out of and is reinforced by a study of the biblical imperatives found in the Prophets and the Gospels.

Young people in many cities are participants in the ethnic antagonisms that surface in their schools and communities. The Bible can be a living word as they endeavor to build bridges through the Christian faith they hold in common. Biblical study and reflection by a youth group, or together by youth groups from different ethnic backgrounds can help pave the way to understanding. The objective is not to find passages through which to discuss tolerance or understanding but to explore together the meanings of their shared faith as a way of mutual understanding. To study and worship together is to be linked in the presence of God.

Vacation Bible school is another opportunity for learning through teaching. Flexible scheduling has presented more opportunities for involving people of all ages. High schoolers as well as adults have jobs, and the services of both are needed as teachers and helpers. Some parishes have late afternoon/early evening intergenerational vacation schools.

Usually adolescents prefer to be in their own groups, yet there are occasions for offering them an opportunity to be full participants in adult study groups. Any such group should be open, because older young people, particularly in small parishes that do not have a separate group for them, may prefer to join the adults if the group is really intergenerational and the program is lively.

Once you find the right occasions for Bible study with young people, you will then be ready to choose a method (see chapter 4). As you discover which method is best for your group, do not ignore the elements of their culture: the cartoons, T-shirt mottoes, music, pastimes, language. These are symbols of their lives, and their mediums for reflection.

This does not mean acceptance of all these symbols; it may mean questioning them. Gobbel writes, "There are times when we are to produce conflict and to create contradictions for adolescents. They must cope with changes. They must develop solutions to tasks. . . .

We are called to help them risk responses and solutions. Our help may demand that we produce conflict, create and identify contradictions, and even contribute to painful and unsettling experiences. The biblical witness will frequently do the same."[13]

FULFILLING POTENTIAL

The intensity of high school study is rarely matched in religious education. Basically our teaching is one of sharing and witness. When the sharing of faith is sincere, young people will respect it. When the sharing of biblical knowledge reveals ignorance and superficiality, young people will infer that their adult teachers do not take biblical understanding seriously enough to study.

Bible is occasionally taught in public secondary schools as a unit within history or literature. These are the parallel fields to which biblical study might be related or compared in terms of content and method, acknowledging different focus and goals. Private schools, and particularly in church-related or other religious schools, will offer serious biblical study. These courses are usually taught by professionals, but not necessarily professionals trained in biblical studies. Teaching Bible may be an assignment for teachers in a related field. Nevertheless, they bring a professional background to their teaching.

In addition, the viewpoints brought by young people need to be recognized as factors facilitating or inhibiting biblical understanding. The basic stance of educational theory is that of scientific inquiry: inductive thinking, research, demonstrating and/or proving statements. This has sometimes resulted in a lesser status for the study of literature, for example, and can make history a search for facts more than an appreciation of the life of a people. This attitude would affect Bible study.

Students bring their own ethical standards to class. These arise from family, school, and culture. Young people often take "values" classes in school, and you need to know what values are discussed and the basis on which they are developed. For example, "values clarification" is a process by which young people are enabled to voice concretely the ethical standards that they believe are right and to assess the extent to which they live up to those standards. This is good, but it does not require any evaluation of those values by an outside standard, such as the Bible, nor does it suggest the possibility of change, although it

---

13. Gobbel et al., *Helping Youth Interpret the Bible,* p. 46.

becomes obvious to the inquirers that it would be to their advantage
to change dangerous practices or beliefs. Recall the study quoted earlier
in this chapter in which young people said that it was good to read
the Bible—but they didn't. Holding a standard without observing it
is not unusual for people at any age.

Political and economic viewpoints brought from home and school
enter into any evaluation of biblical material—for example, the teaching of Torah, the prophets, and Jesus on the meaning of justice. So-
ciocultural understandings are the lenses through which biblical situations are seen. When these inevitable biases are recognized by the
teacher, a basis can be laid for struggling with the implications for
Christian living.

Ethnic background is another viewpoint that each person brings to
the reading of the Bible. Artists have always depicted biblical scenes
with the setting and people familiar to them, usually European. Today
there is biblical art from Asian, African, Hispanic American, and
Native American cultures to help people visualize the Bible in many
contexts. New hymnals include hymns from Asia and Africa.

The work of theologians and biblical scholars in those countries to
interpret what was originally a Middle Eastern text, now adapted to
European culture, into their own cultural history and setting is a
stimulating enrichment for the whole Christian church. Those who
teach young people from cultures different from theirs need to be
aware of this. Caucasians, when the predominant group, need to have
their biblical understandings stretched by becoming familiar with interpretations from other cultures. Think of the possibility of co-teach-
ing with someone from another ethnic background.

In the church setting, teaching is done by volunteers. The difficulty
in finding well-prepared teachers for adolescents arises from the fact
that potential teachers doubt their own adequacy to deal with the
questions and expectations of students. Sharing the faith is important,
but teaching *about* the Bible in order to understand what it is saying
must precede any "responding out of" the text.

Volunteers can also be *amateurs*. The word means a person who
loves what he or she is doing. Communities have highly skilled drama,
choral, and instrumental groups who share a satisfying high level of
performance with their audiences. Bible teachers can also be amateurs.
It entails a preparation different from thoughtful and devotional Bible
reading. Serious study is needed. The next chapter will suggest ways
in which teachers can get the help necessary for them to teach ade-
quately. Admittedly this will take more time than preparing for a
Sunday morning session from a teacher's guide. Such guides do not

help you meet the unexpected questions that arise when adolescents arrive at the intersection of their lives and the biblical Word.

The Bible was originally addressed to adults, but in a culture where children were probably present for much of the reading as well as much of the original telling. Too often we have reduced it to a series of children's stories. Young people need to know that the Bible is addressed to them. Its stories mirror all human experiences. Its teachings touch every human life. Its people, human beings called by God, are like us, and we learn from them. The Bible is the Word of God for growing young adults, the young people in our churches who have turned from childhood toward adulthood and who need the sustenance that the Word of God offers them. To lead and teach these young people is a calling, a responsibility, and a privilege.

The Bible
and Adults

THE ADULT SUNDAY SCHOOL CLASS is a fixture in most congregations and for most Protestant denominations. Sometimes tradition bound, it can also be a freewheeling group that changes subject, leadership, and participants on a regular basis. It can be the most conservative or the most inventive area of parish education. To understand the dynamics and the opportunities, it is necessary to look first at the persons involved.

ADULT DEVELOPMENT

Jean Piaget asserts that beginning around the age of twelve, people can develop the ability to think abstractly, to form and understand concepts, and to reason. This does not assume that everyone will develop the possibility to the fullest, nor does it say anything about individual differences. He does, however, give a foundation on which the objective approach to the study of Scripture is based, and this is an encouragement to those who see the need to enhance laypeople's background in historical and literary criticism as a basis for studying the Bible.

Erik Erikson, continuing his delineation of psychosocial stages, carried the process through the life cycle, describing three stages for the whole of adulthood. His work has been enlarged through a more detailed study of adult stages made by Daniel J. Levenson, using as subjects men living in the area of New Haven, Connecticut. Levenson found transitions between the stages, and he set these in the perspective of stable periods.[1] Another viewpoint is offered by Carol Gilligan in her book *In a Different Voice*.[2] Her specific area of research was in moral development; her subject, girls and women. This was to provide a contrast to the conclusions on moral development made by Lawrence Kohlberg in his studies of boys.

People in Erikson's first stage, that of young adulthood, face the need to develop intimacy; at this stage some will experience negative development into isolation. Intimacy is the ability to relate deeply to another person, as in marriage, to be willing to make commitments and to find a place in the world of work. Levenson provides here an entering stage, ages one to twenty-two, as a transition between adolescence and adulthood. He also posits an age thirty transition followed by a settling down period before entering middle adulthood.

For Erikson, this next stage, beginning at about age forty-five, is one of generativity (verses stagnation). Generativity denotes the nurturing of children toward their adulthood, growth in career decisions and achievements, and entrance into community life. Levenson adds an age fifty transition followed by another settled period, ending in a late adult transition at age sixty.

In Erikson's graph older adulthood has the task of achieving integrity (verses despair), This is a time for reflecting on the whole of life, coming to terms with what has been accomplished as well as with hopes unfulfilled, and finding all of life to be good. Thus settled, a person can enjoy the simplification of life that comes with less work, more leisure, smaller living space, and fewer possessions. It prepares people to accept the final giving up: of physical strength, of mental acuity, of friends, spouse, and self to death. Those who look back on life with only regret, who yearn to continue the lifestyle of middle age (and even of youth), who feel diminished by lessened recognition, and who fight death respond to this stage by despair. With the lengthening of the life span, distinctions are being made in this period. The "young old" are continuing some of their midlife activities, keeping ties with work; those in a mid-old stage are simplifying their lifestyle and are able to look with encouragement on the younger generation who are now in their generative stage; the "old elderly," who may be eighty-five years or older and who with varying degrees of grace accept the slower pace that life imposes on them.

Fowler's faith development stages offer insights here. Many will continue in the synthetic-conventional stage, comfortably affirming

---

1. Daniel Levenson, *The Seasons of a Man's Life* (New York: Alfred A. Knopf, 1982).
2. (Cambridge, Mass.: Harvard University Press, 1982).

the religious community in which they have become established. Others will move into an individuating-reflexive stage, where they become critical of received patterns and want to discover new paths for their personal faith development. Some will later assess these decisions in the light of a new consideration of a more traditional way and find it possible to combine the two in a conjunctive faith. A few may move into a universalizing stage in which they see a broad validity in the life of faith among all people.[3]

One other factor needs to be considered when thinking about adults and the Bible: the total environment in which they live. The world of family brings conflict as well as satisfaction. The world of work brings tensions—job security, promotion—as well as the satisfaction of achievement. The global situation has its own impact as people consider the effect of national and international decisions on their lives.[4]

HOW TO STUDY THE BIBLE

You may need to begin Bible study with inherited patterns. Many adult groups in Protestant churches have for generations met at a traditional Sunday morning hour to study from a quarterly. The curriculum may be the Uniform Lessons Series. Each lesson consists of a Scripture reading, printed in the student's book, an exegetical and expository section giving background to the passage and thoughts for interpretation, and a teaching section with ways to develop a session. Some classes follow the outline, using only the questions suggested and depending on the information offered for interpretation. Their security lies in the familiar.

This approach to Bible study is used illustratively. Reasons for resting in the comfort of the familiar need to be explored. Some people are afraid that if they ask too many questions of the biblical text, particularly those arising from scholarly inquiry, their faith may be threatened. They need to believe that the Word of the Bible is simple and can be easily understood. They find unacceptable the idea that a passage written in a specific context may have one meaning for the people addressed at that time but not have a clear meaning for people today. They may be helped by exegetical study that first illumines the

---

3. *Stages of Faith*. See also Evelyn and James Whitehead, *Christian Life Patterns* (New York: Doubleday & Co., 1979).
4. See Kenneth Stokes, *Faith Development in the Adult Life Cycle* (New York: W. H. Sadlier, 1982), for articles that include perspectives from many disciplines.

text as it might have been heard by the original audience and then asks, What does this say for us? Knowledge does not destroy faith but deepens it. A sensitive leader can help this kind of insight to occur.

The teacher needs to understand the questions explored in chapter 3 about authority, inspiration, and revelation. The class needs to explore the meanings of *truth* and *fact*. Listening and speaking together can bring a realization that exploring viewpoints is an important part of being a study group and that each person can support the other even while differing. Through exploration comes a deeper knowledge of personal convictions, the basis for these convictions, and a knowledge of the factors that can make development, and even change, possible. Many Christians look to the church to be the one secure place in an ever-changing world. It can be, of course, and people need some sense of anchoring. With security in their faith, knowing that God lives and acts continually through them and in the whole world, they may be able to accept dynamic patterns of Bible study. Then the various ways of studying the text, as outlined in chapter 2, can be an enriching experience. Continuous Bible study could enable people to become more flexible in approach, for the years should bring new insights. Looking back on how one heard a story as a child might help adults to realize that when we become adults, we put away childish interpretations.

One approach to Bible study is through topics. Denominational and private publishers offer study guides on a wide variety of topics under the headings of personal religious living, social justice, and ethical concerns—all biblically based. This approach is important when considering the needs of particular age groups, although their concerns overlap. Developing life goals is important to the young adult, while those in middle years have a need to reevaluate their lives, particularly when they are required, or freely choose, to change work or when their marriage is strained. The pervasive question, What is success? raises theological and biblical issues. The way of the cross eventuates in a kind of success not envisioned in Western culture. Issues of personal or social ethics that arouse controversy can be seriously considered in several directions through biblical study.

Another approach is through the study of individual books of the Bible. This gives a group the opportunity to look at the background, explore various critical approaches, read the text in several translations, and "feel into" it. A study course consisting mostly of lectures about the Bible, with illustrations from the Bible, is inadequate. Participants need to read the whole text, to hear it addressed in its time, and to hear it addressed to them. A brief book like Jonah can be an illustration.

Most adults remember a childhood story in which a whale was prominent. A totally new view emerged when they learn about the background against which the story was written and when they hear the story read as adults. Poor Jonah, deprived of shade while he awaits the judgment upon Nineveh, seems amusing. It is less amusing to reflect on the story and see where we ourselves are like Jonah.

Walter Wink has popularized this approach to Bible study. Without repudiating critical Bible study, he nonetheless asserts that this has become the predominant approach, and people concentrate on learning *about* the Bible without ever having to come to terms with what the Bible means in their lives. He insists that there is no "objective" approach to study and no "value-neutral" viewpoint.[5]

His paradigm is a dialectical approach. Begin with the tradition (the biblical passage). The questions it raises help to objectify the passage as well as cause confusion in those who have not really examined it before. This is the process of critical study, and commentaries are consulted. Next the hearers examine the various versions when there is more than one. They are asked to identify with each of the characters. Now their questions center on what was going on in the story. The concluding synthesis comes when hearers are asked, Where are you in this story? Wink's specific illustration is the healing of the paralytic in the Gospels. It becomes apparent that we are each of the characters: friends, paralytic, disciples, critics, with the gamut of emotions conveyed by the story.[6] In a practical manual, Wink outlines a broad range of methods that use not only discussion but painting, writing, and forms of drama such as mime and role play.[7]

There is also a place for the chronological study of the Bible. This is the only way that people can get the historical continuity and the sweep of the action. It requires the kind of concentrated attention that not everyone in a congregation is willing to give. It means attending a serious study group weekly during much of a year and probably continuing over two years or more. Careful preparation is required of the leader, and the group must make a commitment to regular attendance. Several nationally sponsored groups have been found helpful because they stress continuity, require enrollment, have training sessions for leaders, use specially prepared materials, and charge a fee

5. *The Bible in Human Transformation: Toward a New Paradigm for Biblical Study* (Philadelphia: Fortress Press, 1973), pp. 2-4.

6. Ibid., chap. 3, pp. 19ff.

7. *Transforming Bible Study,* 2d ed. (Nashville: Abingdon, 1980).

for participation.[8] Note that this differs from Wink's approach in that it is basically cognitive, centering on content and interpretation. The idea is that one cannot talk in an informed way about the Bible until one has overall knowledge of it as background and that it is better to see each book in the context of the whole before concentrating on the parts.

Another approach is to explore theological beliefs through the Bible. How is salvation used in the Old Testament? How do the New Testament writings answer Jesus' question to the disciples, "Who do you say that I am?" What names are used for God? How is God described? The Bible is not concerned with principles but with God's action. Such a study should uncover the fact that the Bible brings people to affirmations of faith. The confession "Jesus is Lord" is not a concept; it is the victorious statement of those who know, love, and serve him.

Ethical issues are not new—the Bible is filled with such problems. Cain murdered his brother; Jacob cheated his brother; Joseph was sold into slavery by his brothers, who deceived their father. David was convicted of murder and adultery through the prophet's story. The young men at King Nebuchadnezzar's court chose to disobey the king rather than break the covenant. Peter denied Jesus, and Judas betrayed him. Jeremiah warned his people to forsake idolatry or be destroyed.

Do not assume that ethical issues are so modern that they need to be addressed first in terms of a contemporary scenario. This is one approach, using biblical material to suggest ways of viewing the situation. But biblical materials can be found to justify many viewpoints, and it is always possible to reject one or more as not "modern." Alternatively, consider starting with a biblical story or passage. Becoming involved in that situation, learners will have suggestions as to how those people felt, why they responded to the message as they did, and what the outcome might have been. This is a bridge to realizing that little has changed across the centuries: We are like these people, our situation is similar to theirs.

Amos, who came from a Judean village outside Jerusalem, bypassed that city to travel north to Israel, where he described their sin: "You hate the one who reproves in court and despise him who tells the truth. You trample on the poor and force him to give you grain. Therefore, though you have built stone mansions, you will not live in them; though you have planted lush vineyards, you will not drink

---

8. The best known are the Bethel Series, Madison, Wis., and Kerygma, Pittsburgh, Pa. A concise description of these and others may be found in Murray, *Teaching the Bible to Adults and Youth*, pp. 139-148.

their wine. For I know how many are your offenses and how great your sins. You oppress the righteous and take bribes and you deprive the poor of justice in the courts" (5:10-12 NIV). He is a dramatic figure. The result? He was told to go home before the king ordered him to be imprisoned. Read on. Amos promised restoration after Israel repented, for in this view God holds the whole nation to account for the faithlessness of its people. Amos provides a context for dealing with the evils that can become prevalent in any society, describing them, warning of the results, urging repentance and correction, and promising restoration. There are many ways to enlarge the study, beginning with clippings from the daily newspaper. From Torah through the Prophets to the Gospels, justice for all God's people is an emphatic theme.

Another way to study the Bible is in the context of the church year, using the lectionary. There are three readings for each Sunday: Old Testament, epistle, and Gospel. The last forms a connected story from Advent through Pentecost. The others may or may not seem connected. This approach is an enrichment for worship, because people come from Bible study with some thoughts on the Scripture readings, or alternatively, reflect back when a class comes after the service. Because the lectionary gives continuity only to the Gospel story, not to the passages from the Old Testament and epistles, this approach would need to be balanced in other ways by more systematic study of the Hebrew Scriptures, the book of Acts, and the New Testament letters.

OCCASIONS FOR BIBLICAL STUDY

Sunday morning, either before or after the principal morning service, is a popular time for religious education at all age levels. This is a long-standing Protestant tradition, notably in the southern states. The value of this time lies in its convenience, especially for families. The number of people attending may increase if two or more options for approaching Bible study are offered. Possibilities include the type of leadership (lecturer, group leader), the variety of methods (verbal, visual, activity oriented), and a flexible group size (small or large). Large congregations can offer more options, and people have different needs for their learning context.

Many churches, even small ones, distribute weekly calendars that announce at least one weekday opportunity for Bible study. One group may assemble early on a weekday morning for study before work.

Later morning weekly sessions appeal to those who do not work away from home, usually women and retired persons. An evening group offers the opportunity for a serious two-hour study that can include research, discussion, and ways of responding to new learning. In many churches this has become more favored than Sunday morning, which then becomes focused on worship, as has been customary in Catholic and Orthodox churches. Catholic parishes, unfettered by the Sunday morning tradition, have developed innovative structures and employ a wide variety of methods for weekday classes, usually with short-term programs.

The adult Confirmation class can be an important vehicle for biblical teaching in the context of exploring the meaning of the baptismal and confirmation liturgies. In denominations using simpler liturgies, such as Baptist and Christian churches, the biblical meaning of the personal confession of faith in Christ can be probed. The RCIA (Rite of Christian Initiation for Adults) program of the Catholic church, designed for new members and those returning after years of lapsed membership, is a model of ways to participate in the roots of the Christian faith through the medium of a full Baptism and Confirmation liturgy.

It is not necessary for groups to meet for an indefinite length of time. The concentrated study groups mentioned earlier continue for a definite two-year span. Short-term Bible study has a special place for significant seasons such as Advent and Lent. People commit themselves to study for only four or seven weeks, and this seems to be a manageable time span. A carefully planned unit can deepen each participant's Christmas and Easter celebrations.

The size of a group will be related to the methods of study. A featured speaker can hold the attention of a large group. Alternatively, a large group may assemble for an introductory presentation, then disperse into small groups with leaders to probe the passage for its meaning to them. The small group is helpful for people who might like to ask questions or make comments but hesitate to speak in a large group. This gives support as everyone studies together and shares insights. The large group may be better for a video presentation, particularly for a full-length film, and a large screen would be needed. Films often touch the emotions, and people might find it helpful after viewing to respond in small groups. Graphic and writing activities can be offered for either a large or a small group, with suitable space provided for the activities. If sharing the work with others is part of the intention, class members will need to reassemble in small groups. Both large and small groups offer flexibility. With a large enough membership it is possible to have both a large forum and one or more small groups. The small congregation has no alternative. They find that "small is beautiful." The important factor is to make possible the kinds of groups that people with varying ways of expressing themselves find comfortable.

Teacher training sessions can provide another occasion for Bible study. Teachers need this background, which they then translate into approaches appropriate for the age level they teach. Because they are not free to attend Sunday morning classes, they may find that attending a teacher's meeting that gives them this study opportunity enriches their teaching.

Parents' classes are another avenue for learning. Such a study group can help parents understand what their children are learning and encourage them to be full participants in their children's religious education.

Retreats for spiritual growth are also occasions for Bible study (see chapter 9). This might be a two- or three-day retreat or one day of reflection and meditative study. Conference retreats for particular parish groups, such as the parish council (or session or vestry) might well make Bible study an important component to provide a context for their deliberations. Women's, men's, and youth groups similarly have scheduled retreats or conferences that include Bible study as a component.

METHODS OF BIBLE STUDY

Publishers are constantly updating their materials to meet the needs of their markets. Many congregations find these a satisfying source for concise information and practical methods. Others develop their own course outlines and methods for learning. Some Bible study groups base their discussions on books by scholars that are suitably brief or are written in a style that laypeople can grasp. They develop ways to respond to the book by using the Bible references and discussing key issues.

Some groups work from the biblical text alone. They need to be careful that they do not settle for simple answers to profound questions. It is important for them to find the study tools that will help them orient the material to its time and to its meaning for its original audience before they probe its meaning for today. A group with rapport will grow in its ability to share insights and to learn from one another.

Every parish should own basic resource material. Recently published reference books have brief articles in an attractive format. Buying these materials may be costly initially, but reference works are useful for a long time. You will need a good set of maps of biblical lands (not the ones you found in the closet that have been around forty years; they aren't in very good condition). You will also need a biblical commentary, because it gives introductions to books and interpretations of passages; a concordance in which to look up the many references to specific words; and a biblical dictionary or encyclopedia that features brief articles about people, places, and events. You will then need to learn how to use these materials so that they don't sit on a shelf for the next twenty years. An evening get-acquainted session could enrich not only group study but individual study. People would learn to drop by to consult one of the books for a question arising from their own teaching or in personal Bible study.

Some adult classes prefer a lecture or presentation format. This may be done from a traditional quarterly, in which the leader presents the basic material and asks for answers to questions suggested by the text. Frequently this approach is favored in communities that have a college or a theological school from which to draw skilled speakers for lecture series. This approach may be informative and interestingly presented, easily holding the attention of the group. Although this is an excellent way to introduce a unit of study or to draw it to a conclusion, it usually keeps participants from dealing directly with the Bible. They learn *about* the Bible but to not engage it. In a large group, the kind usually attracted to an outside speaker, few dare to express their supposed ignorance by asking a question. When this happens, the group becomes passive participants, unquestioningly absorbing an approach to the book or passage without openly responding. Individuals may in fact be responding internally, brimming with thoughts and questions, but the class dynamic minimizes shared discussion.

Lecture is best used as only one component in Bible study, and it is vital that the question period be conducted well. People should feel free to express their concerns and ask for clarification, and they should have a comfortable rapport with the speaker.

Discussion has been a basic method of Bible study. It requires knowledge in order to have depth. The goal of discussion is comprehension: working toward clarity, eliciting questions for understanding, and sharing opinions that lead to deeper perceptions. Leading discussion is an art that requires openness. The leader needs to be able to receive questions and to encourage wide participation. Discussion does not need to settle anything or come to firm conclusions. It may bring the realization that believers are continually growing in their understanding of the Bible and that life adds to such understanding across the years. The first step in discussion is to ask questions that explore the background of a biblical passage: What is going on in this story? In this way the group can understand the situation, the characters, and the development of the event. The second step is to ask, How do you interpret this story? What do you think was happening for these people? How does it affect you or our time?

The reading or telling of a biblical situation can be the setting for discussion. Imagine the situation depicted in Acts 9, for instance. Saul, recently converted, returned to Jerusalem. When last the Christian congregation heard of Saul it was in connection with the stoning of Stephen, followed by his trip to Damascus to persecute Christians there. Now they were told that he was one of them and was coming to join their group. What do you think they discussed when they heard this news? How do you think they felt? What were their options? When you have read the background in Acts 9:1-25, continue with verses 26-30. You know the answer, of course. But this way of reading it may help you to realize the tense decision making that must have been in back of this brief passage.[9]

The story is basic, whether told or read. Narrative theology becomes concrete in methods of Bible study. Mary Elizabeth Moore, describing a number of approaches to educational method in *Teaching from the Heart,* writes that human beings are capable of imagination and in need of it. Story, she writes, "communicates wholes, the many dimensions of the world, mystery, different perspectives. We ourselves are in the midst of the story."[10] She explains that story communicates in wholes rather than in isolated bits. In story students can discover the flow of time and the interactions among characters and events. If stories are to function in this way, however, they must be full stories, developed with vivid characters and events woven into a whole. "If story functions as a symbol reflecting the interrelated world and fostering our relationships with the world," she writes, "then we need to select stories that reflect many dimensions of the world. . . . We also need stories that point to mystery. We need stories chosen for the largeness of their vision, rather than because of the accuracy of their parts." In conclusion, "Teachers who use narrative method are people who hear stories, gather stories, and tell stories."[11]

---

9. Two volumes of biblical simulations that involve decision-making situations have been written by Donald E. Miller, Graydon F. Snyder, and Robert W. Neff, *Using Biblical Simulations* (Valley Forge, Pa.: Judson Press, 1974).

10. (Minneapolis: Fortress Press, 1991), p. 157.

11. Ibid., pp. 157-58.

Robert Coles, whose work with children was noted earlier, uses story as a basic method of teaching. He does this with medical students, using short stories about doctors. He teaches Harvard undergraduates with stories by Flannery O'Connor and others who have probed ethical issues through powerful narratives. Students can see themselves in these stories. In the introduction to his book *The Call of Stories: Teaching and the Moral Imagination,* he writes, "As I have continued to do psychiatric work with children, I have gradually realized that my teaching has helped that work along—by reminding me how complex, ironic, ambiguous, and fateful this life can be, and that the conceptual categories I learned in psychiatry, in psychoanalysis, in social science seminars, are not the only means by which one might view the world."[12] He concludes (now referring to his college classes), "The moral contradictions and inconsistencies in our personal lives more than resonate with those in our social order, our nation's politics, our culture. As my students keep reminding me, one can go to the Bible itself and find plenty of those same incongruities, those clashes of different or opposing values, ideals."[13] If college students can understand the Bible this way, surely parish groups can also begin their study with the Bible itself.

One of the clearest of writers with a practical approach is Thomas E. Boomershine, who spells out his vision in *Story Journey: An Invitation to the Gospel as Storytelling.* Aware of the tendency to study *about* the Bible, he advocates instead the recovery of the power of story to affect our lives. "The problem is that telling biblical stories is foreign to contemporary experience," he states. "We continue to read Bible stories to children, but the assumption is that once you grow up and learn to think, you will stop telling stories and start telling the truth. Telling the truth means that you will speak in conceptual abstractions."[14] It is often more comfortable to speak in abstractions because they do not touch our lives. As Christians we are expected to let ourselves be confronted by the gospel daily. By becoming involved, by seeing ourselves in the story, we can join with the disciples, who so slowly learned what it really meant to follow Jesus.

Hans-Ruedi Weber's work around the world with Bible study was noted earlier. Much of his book is devoted to descriptions of his various

12. *The Call of Stories: Teaching and the Moral Imagination* (Boston: Houghton Mifflin, 1989), p. 203.
13. Ibid., p. 203.
14. (Nashville: Abingdon, 1988), p. 17. His step-by-step description of storytelling is a helpful guide.

experiments. Bible study leaders will find them suggestive both as outlines to follow or adapt and ideas to translate into their situation.[15]

Study should lead to action. If we ask, What does this passage say to us? the answer given should make a difference in our lives. It may be a personal response affecting how one acts toward the people in one's life. It may mean action in the community or beyond. The action-reflection paradigm for education starts from the thesis that all real learning takes place in the context of activity. For example, a church outreach group might be composed of people who work at a local food bank, assist with a shelter program, or visit families in need. This is participation with others in compassionate deeds. Christians need to take the further step of reflection, where together they ask, Why are we doing this? How is it different from what our partners in service are doing? Those who need help may detect no difference. But through Bible study, together—exploring the meaning, say, of Matt. 25:31-46—they will feel bound together in Christ, for whom they do this service. They know that they are his hands, his feet, to serve his people.

LEADERSHIP OF THE GROUP

Many Bible study groups have a continuing leader. Some have taught the same class for many years. Happy the church that through continuous Bible study has developed a pool of qualified leaders to share teaching duties. Getting individual members to commit themselves to regular attendance may be more difficult to achieve. This is discouraging to a teacher unable to develop continuity in study or cohesiveness in the group.

The pastor is frequently the only theologically trained person in a congregation. In the Jewish community the rabbi, as the term suggests, is the designated teacher. The Presbyterian church names clergy as teaching elders. These teachers need encouragement to continue their study. With the multitude of tasks involved in parish leadership, it is easy to push study aside to a more convenient time. When clergy view teaching Bible study groups as a responsibility, they feel justified in taking time to study. If it seems like personal enrichment, they frequently do not, although they should not feel this way. A parish is doing itself a favor by inviting its leader to teach an occasional unit

---

15. Ibid., part 2, pp. 59-268. Scripts for twenty-five experiments.

of Bible study and to take time for further professional study for which the parish should also provide funding.

Some groups use committee leadership. Several people, working together, plan a year's study. With suggestions from the group, they choose the theme, contact resource people or speakers as needed, designate roles for group members, decide the best times for discussion, and choose the methods for study.

Leaders are responsible for developing resources for study. They should develop a list of outside speakers and resource leaders from the area, get information about videos owned by a church resource center, and gather materials for writing, artwork, and drama or role play.

A Bible study group is interdependent. All leaders are basically resource people, and the response of every participant is important for the learning of all.

THE UNCHURCHED ADULT

The foregoing descriptions of types of groups, methods, and subject matter can suggest possibilities for learning among creative people willing to explore avenues for meeting adult educational needs. They could suggest ways of involving newcomers after they have become interested. Those who are new to the church experience or who are exploring it tentatively, may not consider themselves "religious" but almost certainly would describe themselves as "spiritual."

Where does the Bible fit into this quest for personal spirituality? What role does it play in creating a need for religious community? Do they, as the youth survey mentioned earlier suggested, turn from it as consisting mainly in a set of rules? Are they confused by what they see as complicated theological assertions? Is it possible to draw them through personal involvement as Walter Wink suggests?

Kenneth Stokes, who heads Adult Faith Resources at the University of St. Thomas, Minneapolis, has done extensive study in adult faith development. He notes that there are specific reasons why some people have never been involved in church life and others have renounced church membership; such as an alienating personal experience, personal values they suppose would not be shared by the congregation, or a perception that activities are planned primarily for the parish.[16]

---

16. *Faith Is a Verb: The Dynamics of Adult Faith Development* (Mystic, Conn.: Twenty-Third Publications, 1989), chap. 7, pp. 77-79.

People searching for community, friendships, moral or emotional support frequently find these in small groups. When the parish itself reaches out to serve the wider community, this brings the respect of some who have written off the church as being interested only in its own internal affairs. A personal invitation to attend worship or some other parish event appeals to others.

While some people have felt an emotional estrangement from the church, others remain outside for intellectual reasons. They believe that religiously oriented people have an anti-intellectual bias. A church aware of this bias will find ways to demonstrate that the biblical mode of thinking with heart and mind and soul has its own validity. Feeling and intuition are legitimate tools for interpretation. They can give dimensions to biblical and theological inquiry that earlier critical apparatus did not offer.

The variety of approaches to biblical study with adults in leadership, content, and method offer hope that if church people can explore the meaning of the Bible more creatively, they can invite those outside to a similar life involving exploration.

The Bible
in Worship

Worship is the praise and adoration of God offered by believing people. Every element of a church service contributes to this. The building and every object in it is designed for this purpose. The Greek term *leitourgia* (in English, *liturgy*) means "the work of the people," which explains why the Protestants use the term *worship service* to denote the church's weekly gathering. Orthodox theologian Alexander Schmemann reminds us that "the miracle of the church assembly lies in that it is not the 'sum' of the sinful and unworthy people who comprise it, but the body of Christ. . . . We are the church, we make it up, Christ abides in his members and the church does not exist outside us or above us, but *we are in Christ and Christ is in us*."[1]

In his monumental study *Doxology: The Praise of God in Worship, Doctrine and Life,* Geoffrey Wainright makes it clear that Christians come to understand their faith through liturgy. The basic beliefs, Scripture, prayer, and actions are to be found in this repeated action of the gathered people.[2]

THE BIBLE: BASIC TO CHRISTIAN WORSHIP

Worship is also the primary way through which Christians learn about their faith. Through the centuries it has been the primary form of Christian education. For this reason, classes in which the Bible is studied can never act in place of participation in worship, at any age.

---

1. *The Eucharist: Sacrament of the Kingdom* (Crestwood, N.Y.: St. Vladimir's Seminary Press, 1988), p. 23.
2. (New York: Oxford University Press, 1980).

Classes simply offer a different approach and dimension to what is experienced when hearing Scripture as members of a worshiping congregation.

The early Christian community heard the Hebrew Scriptures, as Jesus and the first disciples did. This included the Torah, the Prophets, and the Psalms. To this they added letters and other writings of the apostles circulating among them. The writer of the letter to the Colossians, for example, concludes with "and when this letter has been read among you, have it read also in the church of the Laodiceans, and see that you read also the letter from Laodicea" (4:16). The passion story was put in written form, and collections of words and deeds from the ministry of Jesus were probably read, decades before they were collected in the Gospels we now have. The early Christian congregations would have expected this, because the reading of Scripture was important in synagogue worship. Note the description of the ceremonial in Luke 4, when Jesus went to the synagogue on the Sabbath "as was his custom": "He stood up to read, and the scroll of the prophet Isaiah was given to him. He unrolled the scroll and found the place where it was written: [Isa. 6:1-2 is quoted]. And he rolled up the scroll, gave it back to the attendant, and sat down. The eyes of all in the synagogue were fixed on him. Then he began to say to them . . ."

Christian monastic communities have long built their daily services around the meditative hearing of Scripture, the chanting of Psalms, and prayer. The Anglican communion has continued this form in the offices of Morning and Evening Prayer. This is the basic content of most forms of Protestant worship, with the addition of other hymns, preaching, prayer, and offertory.[3]

The service of the Word was the part of the liturgy to which the catechumens were admitted in the early centuries. It is still the first part of the eucharistic service.

Continuing the synagogue practice of following a carefully selected series of scriptural readings through the year, the Christian church developed its own lectionary to ensure continuity, variety, and balance in the use of the Bible in worship.

UNDERSTANDING THE LECTIONARY AND ITS USE

The Constitution on the Liturgy, from Vatican II, 1969, revised the lectionary as used by the Roman Catholic church, and those changes

---

3. The best general book giving the history and practice in many traditions is James F. White, *Introduction to Christian Worship,* rev. ed. (Nashville: Abingdon, 1990).

were widely adopted by other Western Christian bodies. It added to the usual epistle and Gospel lessons one from the Hebrew Scriptures and changed from a one-year to a three-year cycle. This greatly increased the amount of Scripture the faithful would hear in the liturgy. The outline, with some modifications, has become the norm for the Episcopal and Lutheran churches and is being used in some denominations that have not usually used a lectionary.[4]

The lectionary is the scriptural expression of the church year. Beginning with the first Sunday in Advent, it follows themes announcing the coming of Christ: his return in glory, John the Baptist, and the announcement to Mary. The Incarnation, both through the Feast of the Nativity and the Epiphany (the visit of the Magi), is followed by the season of his "showing forth"—in baptism, in turning water into wine at the wedding feast, in the Sermon on the Mount, the transfiguration, and other proclamatory moments in the Gospels. We follow Jesus on the road to Jerusalem, climaxed by passion week and completed in the Easter season, where the resurrection appearances become the Sunday readings up to Pentecost. The second half of the year, Pentecost season, is also referred to as "ordinary time," and there is a semi-continuous sequence in the readings.

Epistle readings may be commentary on or teaching from the Gospel. The reading from the Hebrew Scriptures may be parallel to or reflective of the Gospel reading, but there is no intention of reading the Old Testament into the New Testament. One example of a parallel reading is the Passover narrative (Exod. 11:1-14) as the first lesson for Maundy Thursday, followed by the Lord's Supper pericope from 1 Corinthians (11:23-26), and concluding with either Luke's recital of the Last Supper (22:14-30) or John 13:1-15, the washing of the disciples' feet. The lectionary is remembered history. It is the way in which Christians today, gathered for worship, are joined with others throughout almost two thousand years who recounted these same stories to strengthen their faith. Today the many published commentaries on the lectionary, from different publishers and used interchangeably by readers from many denominations, indicate both the commonality of the readings themselves and their widespread use.

The value of this lectionary is that it ensures the hearing of a wide variety of Scripture passages for those who do not regularly read Scripture as a personal practice. Unfortunately this can be said for many Christians. It would be unfair not to recognize that there are

---

4. The Report from the Commission on Common Texts, Revised Common Lectionary 1992 (Nashville: Abingdon Press, 1992).

many for whom daily Bible reading is a practice, that there are Bible study groups in many parishes, and that evangelicals are usually considered more faithful in the practice of personal Bible reading.

Several efforts have been made to involve congregations more personally in Scripture readings. Some congregations have copies of the Bible in the pews so that those who wish can follow the oral reading. Others subscribe to a publication service that provides copies of the Sunday readings, and each person is given a copy on arrival. These may be taken home for use during the week in daily reading, meditation, and prayer.

In many churches, laypeople read the lectionary Scriptures from the lectern, particularly in the Roman Catholic, Episcopal, and Lutheran traditions. The reading of the Gospel is reserved for the ordained priest or pastor or deacon, which in some Protestant traditions symbolizes the ordination responsibility to preach the Scriptures.

This incorporation of laypeople as readers should not be construed to mean that the congregation is otherwise passive. This is emphasized by Schmemann, whose church has often seemed to outsiders to have a liturgy oriented to the celebrants. He writes, "Who is serving . . . is not the clergy, and not even the clergy with the laity, but the Church, which is constituted and made manifest in all fullness by everyone together."[5]

THE BIBLE AND PREACHING

The lectionary features a wide variety of passages for preaching. One hundred fifty-six readings over a three-year period should give ample scope for subject matter. It may require the preacher to base a sermon on some uncomfortable passages. Nobody can accuse the pastor of following personal preferences or prejudices when the passage strikes individual, parish, or societal practice and could condemn or antagonize, no matter how gently approached. Neither the Prophets, the Gospels, nor the epistle writers regarded the sensibilities of hearers when they felt called to speak the word of the Lord. In contrast, the preacher who personally selects the Scripture readings as a basis for a preselected sermon topic must accept responsibility for the choice. This gives some preachers the opportunity to avoid particular issues, as it reinforces the courage of those who deliberately choose to speak a different word.

---

5. *The Eucharist,* p. 88.

The use of the lectionary offers an opportunity for exegetical study. The three-year cycle is popularly known as that of Matthew, Mark, and Luke because these Gospels are the basis in turn for the readings, with John being used at specific points. The book of Acts forms one set of readings during the Easter season. Old Testament and epistle readings are further enrichments for study. This continuity in the lectionary encourages reading and consulting commentaries to enlarge the understanding of passages and entire books.

This emphasis on the exegesis deepens the preacher's expository use of the Bible, as preachers feel responsible for addressing the question of how the Bible affects the life of the congregation. If the pastor is to see the Bible in relation to the daily newspaper or nightly television newscast, then serious exegetical preparation will give depth in answering the question, What is this passage saying to us? Whether the preacher begins with the passage or begins with a life situation is not the question. The conjunction and interweaving of the two in the presence of God with a worshiping congregation provides the dynamism for serious preaching. In a definitive volume on preaching, David Buttrick writes, "If preaching is to form and transform, somehow it must conjoin narrative and naming and thus recover the primal power of word. Preaching is obviously more than talking about the Bible. Preaching, at least Christian preaching, must dare name God in conjunction with the world of lived experience."[6]

Finally, a word on the "children's sermon." I have noticed that when people commend a minister for excellent preaching, they will often refer first to the children's sermon. This indicates to me that simplicity in word and content appeals to the whole congregation, and not only to the children. When children are singled out for one portion of the service and sometimes brought to the front, surrounding the pastor, they become objects rather than subjects in the liturgy. The attention of the rest of the congregation is focused on the children's response, sometimes with gently appreciative laughter. This makes children something less than full participants.

The children's sermon is usually found in two forms. One is the "object lesson," in which some concrete object is meant to stand for an abstract idea. Children, being practical creatures, remember the object which is, after all, the most vivid part of the presentation. The presumed "religious" teaching is therefore lost. The other form is story: either a biblical story or an experience-oriented story in which

---

6. *Homiletic: Moves and Structures* (Philadelphia: Fortress Press, 1987), p. 18.

the listener identifies with persons in a situation with implications for the Christian life.

One Sunday children gathered around their pastor for a vividly told story about a boy who, envious of his sister's birthday, ran his fingers through the icing on the cake, then went to her room and smashed a favorite toy. Mother, discovering these actions, wisely expressed sympathy for his feelings but not his actions. She showed him how together they could repair the cake and indicated that he could use his money to replace the toy. Both children and adults in the congregation could understand envy and the results. They too face similar situations. But, alas, the pastor, unwilling to trust the effect of her own excellent story telling, continued by explaining what was wrong. Moralizing ruined the impact. The rational explanation overcame the real feeling that the story itself had left. If response was needed, the questions to be asked, softly, were: Is there anything you would like to say about the story? Has anything like this ever happened to you? Would you like to tell us what you did? "Perhaps when you get to your class," the pastor might have said, "you will want to talk more about it." Such questions will register with adults also.

The story used should be either a retelling of a narrative from the lectionary for the day or an implication from the reading. In this way the adult congregation will already have an introduction to the sermon.

Better still, the one sermon, following the Scripture readings of the day, should be brief and carefully crafted to retell the biblical situation. Illustrate it in stories from people—men, women, and children—and suggest ways in which God is speaking to that congregation. (Someday note the sermon illustrations and see if they do include everyone. I find that children rarely appear as real people, and women's experiences are seldom heard.)

Women have pressed for the use of more inclusive language in biblical translations. The first effort was made in *An Inclusive Language Lectionary*.[7] This was a thoroughgoing revision and its introduction explains the recasting. For example, *Lord* is translated "Sovereign One." Women are listed among the ancestors (not "forefathers"). The New Revised Standard Version, published in 1989, changes the generic use of *man* to an inclusive word such as *people* and changes the pronoun *he* to *they*. It makes no changes in the pronouns referring to God. Similar revisions have been made for a Revised New English Bible

---

7. (New York: Division of Educational Ministry, NCC, USA, Year A 1983), Years B and C followed.

and a Revised Jerusalem Bible. The Book of Common Prayer has made similar changes in the Psalter.

THE PSALMS IN WORSHIP

The Psalms keep us in continuity with our roots in the synagogue service. Many were written for liturgical use. The reader can almost see the processions that accompanied these hymns and hear the acclamations. The use of the Psalms is integral to the daily monastic offices, as well as to Morning and Evening Prayer in the Anglican tradition. The Roman Catholic, Lutheran, and Episcopal eucharistic rites incorporate a portion of a psalm between the Old Testament and epistle readings. Protestant churches frequently use a responsive reading that may be from the Psalms or may include prose passages from the Bible. Canticles, used in the daily offices, include biblical and early church songs, from the Song of Moses (Exodus 15) to the Song of the Redeemed (Revelation 15). The *Te Deum* (You are God) and the *Gloria in Excelsis* (Glory to God in the highest) are the only canticles not directly from Scripture and probably date from the fourth century. The canticles take up twelve pages in the Book of Common Prayer.

Frequently the Psalms are sung to simple melodies—chants—which may be described as sung speech. In congregations, one phrase from the psalm of the day may be sung by the people, alternating with the verses sung by the cantor or choir. The Genevan and Scottish psalm tunes in the Reformed tradition are rhymed versions of the Psalms set to music. "All People That on Earth Do Dwell" is the most familiar.

Some psalms have long been a part of Christian liturgy because of their associations. Psalm 51, with its clearly penitential mood, is used on Ash Wednesday. Psalm 22 is appropriate for Good Friday, beginning as it does with the words "My God, my God, why have you forsaken me." It continues, "They pierce my hands and my feet"; "They divide my garments among them; they cast lots for my clothing."

Dietrich Bonhoeffer, theologian of the German confessing church during the time of Hitler, wrote of the Psalms:

> The *Man* Jesus Christ, to whom no affliction, no ill, no suffering is alien and who yet was the wholly innocent and righteous one, is praying the Psalter through the mouth of his Church. The Psalter is the prayerbook of Jesus Christ in the truest sense of the word. He prayed the Psalter and now it has become his prayer for all time. Now do we understand how the Psalter can

be prayer to God and yet God's own Word, precisely because here we encounter the praying Christ? Jesus Christ prays through the Psalter in his congregation. His congregation prays too. The individual prays. But here he prays insofar as Christ prays within him, not in his own name, but in the name of Jesus Christ.[8]

BIBLICAL AFFIRMATIONS IN CONGREGATIONAL WORSHIP

The Ten Commandments are a teaching used in worship. In some traditions they are affirmed weekly; in others, repeated at special times, as during Lent. The Commandments may be repeated in unison. Or the leader may say the words, the congregation making a response: "Amen" to denote their acceptance of the words; "Lord, have mercy" as a plea to be enabled to keep them. Today the basic statements are frequently used in shortened form. Congregations also use the summary of the Law found in Matt. 22:37, 39; Mark 12:29-31; Luke 10:27. These are quotations from Deut. 6:4-5, the Shema, the basic affirmation of Jewish faith, combined with Lev. 19:18.

The two historic creeds are composed of biblical affirmations but are not always direct quotations from the Bible. The Apostles' Creed, which reached its present form in the eighth century, has been used as a baptismal creed in the Western church. Today it is the basic formulary of faith in some denominations, whether used weekly or occasionally. The name *Apostles' Creed* comes from the tradition that it contains the basic belief of the early church. Because it is phrased in the first person singular, it is appropriate for making the personal confession of faith in Baptism or Confirmation.

The Nicene Creed, formulated by the bishops at the Ecumenical Council at Nicea in 325, was designed to express the church's basic belief after Christianity had been given official status in the Roman Empire. It is written in the first person plural as an expression of the faith of the community. The Episcopal and Lutheran churches use it in the Eucharistic service; the Roman Catholic church does not require its weekly use. The second section, on Jesus Christ, is more elaborate than that in the Apostles' Creed because it was written to express the church's theological understanding of his relationship to God after a long period of controversy over this issue. It should be remembered that these are confessions of faith, stating I (or we) believe *in,* that is,

---

8. *Life Together* (New York: Harper & Row, 1954), pp. 46-47.

have faith and trust in God. They are not only statements of intellectual assent to what I (we) believe *about* God.

Because of their biblical content, they deserve serious study, not only by those preparing to affirm the creed in Baptism or Confirmation, but by all believers, continually maturing in their understanding of who God is and how God acts. Geoffrey Wainwright writes,

> The use of creeds, whose substance goes back to apostolic times and whose precise formulations go back to patristic times, has allowed successive generations of Christians to find their identity in a Church to which its Founder is believed to have promised his abiding presence and support until the end of time. When the believer confesses his baptismal faith, he is being initiated into a people of God which has a historical identity undergirded by the Christ who is "the same yesterday, today and forever." As long as the believer goes on recapitulating his confession, he may be assured of his own identity in the identity of the Christian people.[9]

Brief sentences from the Bible are used throughout a service of worship. The Psalms are a rich resource for the call to worship, as are the greetings of Paul to the churches. There are numerous quotations to introduce the offertory, beginning with that in Acts 20:25, when Paul is quoted as encouraging the Ephesian elders to care for those in need, saying, "Remember the words of the Lord Jesus, for he himself said, 'It is more blessed to give than to receive.' " Paul's closing words in letters suggest words for benedictions, as does the priestly blessing found in Num. 6:24, beginning "the Lord bless you and keep you." Occasional versicles and responses may be simple phrases from the Bible. "Peace be with you" (John 20:19), the *Sanctus,* "Holy, Holy, Holy," comes from Isa. 6:1–4 and is echoed in Rev. 4:8. "Blessed is he who comes in the name of the Lord. Hosanna in the highest" is from the Psalm Sunday narrative, Matt. 21:8–9. Go through your service of worship and you will notice others, perhaps some that you have so taken for granted that you never thought of their source.

THE BIBLE IN PRAYER

The Lord's Prayer, the Our Father, has been called the prayer of the church. In each of the places in the Gospels where it is recorded, the

---

9. *Doxology,* p. 190.

setting is a gathering of the disciples. Luke 11:1-4 reads, "He was praying in a certain place, and when he ceased, one of his disciples said to him, 'Lord, teach us to pray, as John taught his disciples.' " Jesus' reply was, "When you pray, say 'Our Father.' " Although it does not conclude with the doxology, Matthew's version is also set in a gathering of the disciples. The Sermon on the Mount, a long teaching discourse (chapters 5-8) begins, "When Jesus saw the crowds, he went up the mountain; and after he sat down, his disciples came to him. Then he began to speak, and taught them." After some words about how not to pray, he says, "Pray then in this way: Our Father . . ." (6:9-13). So far the prayer is identical to that in Luke, but a footnote in recent translations reads, "Other ancient authorities add, in some form, 'For the kingdom and the power and the glory are yours forever. Amen.' " This is the doxology, praise to God, which was integral to Jewish liturgical prayer. As such, it brings a liturgical character to the Lord's Prayer and lifts it beyond individual petition, although the "we" form has already done so.

In using the Lord's Prayer regularly in worship, therefore, we are affirming a link with the earliest Christian communities, and with the doxological ending we indicate our roots in Jewish liturgical prayer.

Pastors who are rooted in Scripture will frequently use biblical phrases in the pastoral prayer, thereby deepening and enriching this vital action of the worshiping community. The collects used in some churches are also replete with biblical allusions. A study group could track down such allusions and references and so become aware of the richness of the liturgical tradition through its biblical sources.

The call to worship may itself be a prayer, as "Let the words of my mouth and the meditation of my heart be acceptable to you, O Lord, my rock and my redeemer" (Ps. 19:14). Some preachers use this before beginning the sermon. As a prayerful benediction there is "May the God of hope fill us with all joy and peace in believing through the power of the Holy Spirit" (Rom. 15:13).

THE BIBLE IN MUSIC

It is written in 1 Chron. 13:8 that when the ark was brought to Jerusalem, "David and all Israel were dancing before God with all their might, with song and lyres and harps and tambourines and cymbals and trumpets." Now there is joyous praise in music! More modestly, the young Christian church at Ephesus is admonished to "be filled with the Spirit, as you sing psalms and hymns and spiritual songs among yourselves, singing and making melody to the Lord in your hearts" (5:19). The Colossians are told "with gratitude in your hearts sing psalms, hymns, and spiritual songs to God" (3:16).

Singing in praise and thanksgiving to God is integral to the religious expression of biblical people. This has already been noted in the section on the Psalms, which include not only those songs to be found in the book by that name but others throughout the Bible. The first chapters of Luke's Gospel include several early Christian hymns: Mary's Song (1:46-55), Zachariah's (1:68-79), and Simeon's (2:29-32). It has been suggested that the book of Revelation describes a heavenly liturgy, filled as it is with hymns of praise: "You are worthy, our Lord and God, to receive glory and honor and power, for you created all things, and by your will they existed and were created" (4:11).

The early church did not feel confined to scriptural words for hymns. The faith and doctrine of the church was expressed in its hymnody, which the writers supposed echoed biblical teaching. One of the earliest in our hymnals is "Of the Father's Love Begotten" by Prudentius (348-410?). As an expression of the gathered community, hymns were a source of mutual strengthening, as they are today.

The use of biblical texts and allusions in modern hymnody came with the Reformation. Martin Luther's Christmas hymn "From Heaven High" echoes the angelic song in Luke. "From Deepest Woe a Cry to Thee" is based on Psalm 139. The well-known "A Mighty Fortress Is Our God" is based on Psalm 46.

The Reformed tradition produced psalm paraphrases in Geneva, Scotland, and England. "I to the Hills Will Lift Mine Eyes," paraphrased from Psalm 121, is from *The Psalms of David in Meeter* (dated 1650). This tradition has continued. The indexes of hymnals list the Psalms used in hymnody. You will find numerous entries under the headings of authors or translators and sources. Under composers, arrangers, and sources for hymns you will find references to the older psalm tunes.

To understand the importance of hymnody as one avenue for strengthening biblical faith, make a study of hymns used by your congregation. Find the biblical references and allusions. Look at some new hymns you may not have used. Several denominations have published new hymnals recently, and there are a number of contemporary writers expressing their faith through hymnody.

As noted earlier, the hymns of Brian A. Wren appear in many recent hymnals. Struggling with the question of gender pronouns, metaphors, and analogies, he has explored the possibilities in a book significantly titled from the passion chorale *What Language Shall I Borrow?*

God-Talk in Worship: A Male Response to Feminist Theology.[10] He eschews general terms such as Creator, Redeemer, and Sustainer in favor of the personal: friend or lover. He points out that the maleness of Jesus included characteristics and actions that many cultures have considered female. He uses *he* and *she* interchangeably in referring to God. Wren's thinking has been made concrete in his hymns (some are used illustratively in the book) and represents the new wave of hymnody now appearing in congregational worship.

Liturgical music is that composed for use in the service of worship. In addition to hymns, there are settings for the various responses used. Churches that use ancient hymns such as the *Gloria* and the *Sanctus* have incorporated these and others, with several musical settings, in a specific section of their hymnal designated as service music. Great composers, classical and modern, have done settings for the mass, the eucharistic liturgy, and these are regularly performed in churches that have choirs skilled enough to learn them. A study of several such settings offers insights into how the style of a particular composer influenced the way in which the words to the liturgy were understood.

The choir anthem is also a part of the liturgy. Some traditions permit only words that are scriptural or based on the liturgical texts. This has produced a rich literature of musical settings for psalms, biblical hymns, and other parts of the service. Being a member of a choir is an education in understanding the Christian faith. A children's or youth choir can be an educational as well as a spiritual experience for participants if the director or a co-teacher takes time to help children explore and understand the words they are singing and to grasp the way in which the music expresses the words.

Probably the best-known choir anthems are the lectionary-based cantatas from the pen and the deeply Christian experience of Johann Sebastian Bach (1685-1750). Solo and recitative tell the story; the chorale expresses the response of the congregation. In "Now Comes the Gentiles' Savior" for the first Sunday in Advent, the majestic overture with chorus is followed by a recitative with words from Revelation: "Behold, I stand at the door and knock" (bass solo because these are the words of the Lord), followed by the response of the soul (soprano) and the joyous chorale ending in the hymn "How Brightly Beams the Morning Star." For Bach, this Sunday, focusing on the return of Christ in glory, is cause for joy.

The Passion according to St. Matthew and the Passion according to St. John by Bach are monumental works. Biblical study of the

---

10. (New York: Crossroad, 1989).

passion through this interpretation could be a strengthening experience for a Lenten study group (see also chapter 4). The St. John Passion is shorter, opening and closing with magnificent choruses that express the special quality of John's interpretation of the gospel. It could be used as the setting for a Good Friday service with only the addition of the Gospel readings and prayers before each of the six sections. Recordings have made great music widely available for listening and study.

THE BIBLE IN SACRAMENTS AND INITIATORY RITES

The book of Acts says that those baptized on the day of Pentecost "devoted themselves to the apostles' teaching and fellowship, to the breaking of bread and the prayers" (2:42). This has been interpreted to mean that participation in the Lord's Supper was integral to worship in the earliest times. The oldest written description available is in *The First Apology* of Justin Martyr (died ca. 165). After prayers together, and the greeting of one another with a kiss, the bread and cup of water mingled with wine are presented to the president. Praise and thanksgiving are offered to God. The words of institution are repeated, and the "eucharistized" bread and wine-with-water are given to each by the deacons and carried to those who are absent.[11]

The words of Jesus at the Last Supper are basic to this observance and celebration. They are found in the first three Gospels and in Paul's first letter to the Corinthians (11:23-26). In some traditions this is an observance in memory of Christ's self-offering. In others it is the weekly remembrance of the resurrection appearances to disciples and the affirmation that the risen Christ is in the midst of this present congregation. The Greek word *anamnesis* means more than simple memory. It has the connotation of making present. The remembered past is vitally reenacted in this moment and among this congregation. This is the force of the threefold time reference with which Paul concludes his recital: "For as often as you eat this bread and drink this cup, you proclaim the Lord's death until he comes."

Some liturgies, following Justin Martyr's thanksgiving "at length," give thanks for God's work in creation, in the people of Israel, and the incarnation in Jesus. After the Last Supper recital, the petition is made that the Holy Spirit come upon the gifts to transform them. So

---

11. Bard Thompson, ed., *Liturgies of the Western Church* (Cleveland: World Publishing, 1962), pp. 3-10.

the prayer surrounding the dominical words also affirm the biblical ties of these people of God. In order to understand the liturgy fully, a study group can seek the biblical references and allusions. They will find their congregation deeply linked to ancient roots. Gregory Dix, in his seminal book *The Shape of the Liturgy,* sums it up:

> The outlines of that ritual pattern come down to us unchanged in the christian practice from before the crucifixion, the synaxis from Jesus' preaching in the synagogues of Galilee, the eucharist proper from the evening meals of Jesus with His disciples. The needs of a christian corporate worship gradually brought about their combination. The whole has a new meaning fixed for all time in the Upper room. But the form of the rite is still centred upon the Book on the lectern and the Bread and Cup on the table as it always was, though by the new meaning they have become the Liturgy of the Spirit and the Liturgy of the Body, centring upon the Word of God enounced and the Word of God made flesh.[12]

Baptismal liturgies vary. The simplest, asking only the question, Do you accept Jesus Christ as your Lord and Savior? still has biblical roots to be explored. There are several brief confessions of faith and baptismal formulas in the New Testament to invite serious probing, such as Acts 8:38 (footnoted in recent translations) and Acts 16:30-33. The Roman Catholic and Eastern Orthodox liturgies are filled with symbolism and the continuation of ancient practices. These have their basis in biblical and historic tradition. Those being baptized, or parents and sponsors of young children, need an opportunity to study the meaning of Baptism through its biblical roots: the baptism of Jesus, his reference to disciples being baptized with his baptism (Matt. 20:22), Paul's reference to disciples being baptized into Jesus' death (Rom. 6:3), and being baptized into one body (Rom. 12:13). When Baptism is given without this background, new Christians are deprived of the possibility of fully understanding who they are.[13]

Scripture can be similarly used in the Confirmation or church membership service. Here the emphasis is on what it means to give allegiance

---

12. (London: Dacre Press, Adam and Charles Black, 1945), p. 743.
13. The relationship of learning to liturgy is enunciated by Gwen Kennedy Neville and John H. Westerhoff III in their book *Learning through Liturgy* (New York: Seabury Press, 1978); and in John H. Westerhoff III and William H. Willimon, *Liturgy and Learning through the Life Cycle* (New York: Seabury Press, 1980).

to Christ as Lord or to become fully integrated into the body. Identifying with the experiences of being a disciple as recounted in the Gospels is important. In addition, we like them become apostles, people "sent forth" so the experiences of those who proclaimed the faith as told in the Acts of the Apostles are essential for our self-understanding. The Orthodox church uses the whole initiatory rite with infants. There is discussion among some Christian bodies today about the place of Confirmation. Liturgical scholar James White takes issue with the popular understanding of Confirmation. "Instead of being reunited to baptism," he writes, Confirmation was changed by the Reformation "into a didactic experience expressed as a graduation exercise for those who had mastered the catechism. Much of Christian education has been built on such a dubious solution."[14] If this seems harsh, it may also suggest that further biblical study can enrich the meaning of Christian initiation.

THE BIBLE IN PASTORAL RITES

The church has recognized in marriage Jesus' assertion of God's creation: "So God created humankind in his image, in the image of God he created them; male and female he created them" (Gen. 1:27 and 5:1-2). Jesus added, "They are no longer two, but one flesh. Therefore what God has joined together, let no one separate" (Mark 10:6-9 and Matt. 19:4-6). The Book of Common Prayer affirms that Christ's presence and first miracle at a wedding in Cana of Galilee "signified to us the mystery of the union between Christ and his Church."[15] This invites the pastor to offer consideration of the biblical meaning of marriage in discussion with the couple about to be married. Some marriage liturgies today provide for the inclusion of readings from Scripture. When the couple are given the opportunity to choose the readings, they engage in Bible study as they consider the passages that might have the deepest meaning for them.

The memorial service or burial rite has traditionally been one of Scripture readings and prayers. Great passages from the Psalms, Gospels, and epistles lift up the hearts of family and friends: "I am the resurrection and the life, says the Lord"; "I know that my redeemer lives." The eucharistic service provides special lectionary readings for the day. Family and friends are comforted and sustained as believers

---

14. *Introduction to Christian Worship,* pp. 180-81.
15. (New York: Seabury Press, 1977), p. 423.

reaffirm their faith together. The biblical material in these services can be helpful for pastors counseling a family. They would be basic material for study groups focusing on the meaning of dying and death.

Ordination is another service with biblical roots in the laying on of hands for special offices. A hymn sometimes used at ordinations for the ministry says, "Elijah's mantle on Elisha cast." Laypeople need to know the background for this event, which, in some traditions, has an indelible quality. There are a number of references in Scripture to the laying on of hands. Moses commissioned Joshua to become his successor (Deut. 34:9); seven men from the Greek-speaking believers were chosen for service to their community by the laying on of hands of the Twelve (Acts 6:6). Peter and John laid their hands on a group of newly baptized Samaritan believers and they received the Holy Spirit (Acts 8:17). The laying on of hands was also used for healing.

Confession, or the rite of reconciliation, includes biblical words of assurance and penitence: "Blot out my transgressions. Cleanse me from my sin," prays the psalmist (51:1, 2); "Christ Jesus came into the world to save sinners" (1 Tim. 1:15).

Services of healing are held in many traditions, relying on the Gospel accounts of Jesus' healings. James 5:14-15 urges, "Are any among you sick? They should call for the elders of the church and have them pray over them, anointing them with oil in the name of the Lord. The prayer of faith will save the sick."

Several special services of worship have become popular in recent years. The service of lessons and carols, well known from the recording at King's College Chapel, Cambridge, combines Scripture readings and Christmas music. Readers include young choir members and distinguished elders. Study the order of the passages as well as the content and the relationship to Christmas. The Tenebrae service for Holy Week is constructed around a series of fourteen readings from the Psalms, each reading followed by a response. Candles are extinguished after each reading, and finally the topmost candle, signifying Christ, is removed and the church darkened. Then that light alone is returned to its place. These psalms and responses form a meditative background for study and reflection during Lent and Holy Week. More recent Tenebrae services are built around the events of the night preceding the passion (Luke 22:39—23:25).

The Great Vigil of Easter, held sometime after sundown on the Saturday preceding Easter Sunday, opens with a series of biblical readings from Genesis through Zephaniah. Study and reflect on each to understand why they are placed in this setting as the first celebration of the resurrection.

FORM AND CONTENT IN WORSHIP

Liturgy is drama. Hans Ruedi Weber explains,

> The Bible as a written manuscript developed alongside the Bible
> as a liturgical enactment. The recollection and oral traditions of
> the Exodus event led both to its liturgical re-enactment in the
> Jewish Passover feast and to the writing down of the Exodus
> traditions. . . . Throughout the centuries, and probably even
> today, the majority of Christians—Orthodox, Roman Catholic,
> and Protestant—know the biblical message not from their own
> reading of the Bible-book, but from participating in the biblically
> shaped liturgical drama.[16]

In some traditions the delivery of the sermon may be the most
dramatic portion. In others the music, by choir and/or congregation.
In still others the eucharistic rite. In one way or another, the whole
congregation participates in this drama, by their presence and their
attentiveness as well as by their vocal or other physical actions. In
some traditions dance or a play have further conveyed the drama. This
survives in Protestant practice principally in terms of the Christmas
pageant, although this frequently takes the form of a charming pre-
Christmas celebration by the youngest members of the congregation.
While lacking the sense of wonder conveyed by the Gospel story, it
gives the congregation some sense of reenacting the event.

Much of the symbolism in a church building refers to the biblical
text. The cross is the most central symbol. Each particular design
expressed an interpretation of the passion and resurrection of the Lord,
from the tortured figure on a medieval crucifix to a simple contemporary cross. Each conveys some aspect of the story that meditation
and study in the presence of the cross will reveal. The placing of the
Bible is symbolic—on the pulpit or a lectern; whether carried in pro-
cession or read from among the congregation. The setting of the altar
or table and the communion vessels interpret the rite. Vestments represent preaching (the Geneva robe) or priestly functions (eucharistic
vestments). Both the form and the setting of the baptismal font is
significant. That used for Baptism by immersion is different from one
used with a simpler rite. Placing the font at the entrance to the church
signifies Baptism as the entrance into the Christian life.

---

16. *Experiments with Bible Study,* p. 29.

Biblical antecedents for the furnishing of the church are found in the Exodus accounts of the tabernacle and the account of Solomon's temple in 2 Chronicles. Form and function are combined in furnishings that are reminders of the tradition while also being of practical use. Stained-glass windows have reminded people of biblical stories since the late Middle Ages. Churches that have these should give people opportunities to explore their meaning and to compare the artists' work with the biblical stories being depicted.

Language is a symbol system, and the language of worship has significance. The concern today for inclusive language—so that *man* is not used as a generic term for human beings, for instance—has brought about many changes in liturgies and texts, including, as mentioned already, the New Revised Standard Version of the Bible (1989). In *Christ in Sacred Speech: The Meaning of Liturgical Language,* Gail Ramshaw-Schmidt explores the grammar, syntax, and metaphors of liturgy. She sets a twofold task: to free up traditional metaphors to speak their own riches (shepherds are not always male; Rachel was a shepherd) and to incorporate more feminine metaphors into liturgy.[17] She writes significantly, "Our first step in affirming God's name must be our humble realization that no human being can fully know the name of God or can finally and completely call down God's mysterious being. . . . This is how we name God, with these names, around the mystery of Christ."[18]

The Christian congregation's worship is an expression of its biblical faith, in all its words and actions: through hymn, Scripture, sermon, prayer, and Eucharist. The richest liturgies are those that most fully embody and convey this Word of God.

---

17. (Philadelphia: Fortress Press, 1988), pp. 55-56.
18. Ibid., p. 44.

The Bible in
Spiritual Development

THE BIBLE HAS LONG BEEN A SOURCE OF STRENGTH for individuals. They turn to its pages in times of joy and thanksgiving. They seek strength in time of need. They seek reassurance when events are puzzling. They seek comfort in time of sorrow. When it is difficult to forgive, people recall the disciples' question, "How often?" and Jesus' response, "Up to seventy times seven"—more than you can count. The parable of the good Samaritan reminds people to help according to need, not according to who is in need. The parable of the prodigal son reassures people of God's restorative love. Psalm 23 is murmured by individuals in moments of extremity and by congregations for mutual support.

The Hebrew Scriptures are frequently quoted in the New Testament. Paul's much-quoted statement, "The one who is righteous will live by faith" is from Hab. 2:4. Indeed the book of Romans, where Paul interprets his Jewish heritage within his experience of the gospel, is filled with quotations from Hebrew Scripture: Genesis, Deuteronomy, Psalms, Hosea.

CLASSIC FORMS OF MEDITATION

Meditation is a form of prayer in which an individual or group reflects silently on words, ideas, or pictures in the presence of God. The Society of Friends practices silence as the basis for its congregational worship. Two long-held devotional traditions describe biblical forms for meditation.

Ignatius of Loyola (1491–1556) developed a form of meditation based on picturing biblical stories. Although the method itself includes many steps, its practical application comes from its visualization.[1] Think for a moment about the story of Zacchaeus (Luke 19:1-10). As you read the story, or as someone reads it to a small group, mentally place yourself among the crowd. The action swirls around you. You are in Jericho, the ancient oasis city at the Jordan River, the turning point for those going up through the wilderness hills to Jerusalem. Jesus and his closest disciples are walking through its crowded streets. (He had already healed a blind man begging at the roadside outside the city.) Now he suddenly pauses. Why? He looks up into a sycamore tree, and all eyes follow the look. You make out the form of a man in the tree. What does he look like? What is the expression on his face? Would he have been too small to see over the crowd, or was he just hoping for a better view? What do you, as one of the crowd, do when you see him? Are you astonished? Do you laugh appreciatively at his forethought or derisively at his boldness? Now Jesus speaks, and you follow his words. They made Zacchaeus happy, but how do you feel? Do you share the response of the crowd, or do you have different feelings toward this man so determined to see Jesus (but not to be seen). Respond to Zacchaeus's answer to Jesus. How do you feel as Zacchaeus walks beside Jesus while you and the others follow toward Zacchaeus's house?

With visualization this Bible story, which you have heard since childhood, will take on a depth of meaning you might not have considered. You will understand how it feels to be one of the crowd. You will have been caught up in a confrontation between Jesus and a sinner who could not resist responding to his call. Here is the special power of a visualized Bible story. There are many more in the Gospels for the deepening of your spiritual life.

Another classical form of meditation is the use of the Jesus prayer.[2] This is a practice of Eastern Orthodox monastic communities. It became more widely known through a nineteenth-century book, *The Way of a Pilgrim,* in which an itinerant holy man uses this as his basic form of devotion and teaches it to others.[3] The words are "Lord Jesus Christ, Son of the Living God, have mercy on me, (a sinner)." This

---

1. Louis Puhl, trans., *The Spiritual Exercises of St. Ignatius Loyola* (Westminster, Md.: Newman Press, 1951).
2. Per-Olof Sjogren, *The Jesus Prayer* (London: SPCK, 1974; 1st American ed., Philadelphia: Fortress Press, 1975).
3. R. M. French, trans., *The Way of a Pilgrim* (London: SPCK, 1972; New York: Seabury Press, 1972).

is a Christian mantra, for it is intended to be used repeatedly, simply to bring one into the presence of God. The words merge, and the cry to God becomes a part of the self. For this reason it has been referred to as "the prayer of the heart." Recent years have brought a renewed interest in forms of meditation and a discovery by Westerners of methods of prayer from Hinduism and Buddhism. Christians have been recovering their own ancient contemplative heritage, and the Jesus prayer is one form. It brings into focus a basic affirmation of the Gospels, combining as it does the opening statement of Mark's Gospel, "The beginning of the good news of Jesus Christ, the Son of God," with the cry of the two blind men (Matt. 20:29), "Lord, have mercy on us, Son of David," a phrase found in some form in three Gospels.

Although you probably do not think of the life of prayer in the same way as you think of education, learning is nevertheless taking place. People learn new forms of prayer, new ways of entering more deeply into their life with God. They also gain a new perspective on the Bible, a deeper way of understanding its meaning. Learning can take place even when it is not the stated objective of an activity.

POPULAR FORMS THAT USE THE BIBLE DEVOTIONALLY

Millions of people use daily devotional guides. Some are used largely by members of the denomination publishing the guides, but others have a wide readership. The usual format is designed with one page for each day of the month, although some may cover a three-month (one quarter) period. The page is headed by a Bible verse and may suggest reading a longer passage. This is followed by a brief interpretation of the verse. The page is concluded with a short prayer. Such devotional guides are designed for individual use. They can also be used as the opening worship for small groups, and their use may be extended so that the passage and meditation become the catalyst for the group itself to enter more deeply into the meaning of Scripture and prayer.

More comprehensive devotional guides, sometimes by well-known writers, may be designed for a year of readings or may simply express the writer's thoughts in whatever number of pages seems needed. These may be more exegetical than the smaller-format daily devotional guides because the writers are not confined by space limits.[4]

---

4. See John Baillie, *A Diary of Private Prayer* (New York: Charles Scribner's Sons, 1952); Frederick Buechner, *An Alphabet of Grace* (San Francisco: Harper & Row, 1984); Madeleine E'Engle, *The Irrational Season* (New York: Farrar, Straus & Giroux, 1977).

Devotional guides for Advent and Lent are popular. Lent has long been a season when people take time to deepen the spiritual life, so the Lenten guide has been a staple both for denominational and general publishers of popular religious books. Advent guides have seen increasing use as individuals, families, and small groups explore themes for the weeks preparatory to the Christmas season.

Here also education is taking place. Indeed for some people it may be the most consistent form of biblical learning. Not only are themes explored in brief exegesis, but those special seasons of the Christian year, Advent and Lent, become deepened in ways that counteract the persistent messages of the surrounding culture. When devotional guides encourage people to read the material surrounding the brief biblical verse of the day, they further enrich people's knowledge of the text.

THE BIBLE ALONE AS SPIRITUAL GUIDE

Many people turn to the Bible itself without further commentary as part of their spiritual practice. Some follow a Bible reading guide. Some use the Sunday lessons or the daily lectionary as their guide. Others choose a book, reading a section or a chapter each day. When this is balanced at other times by the kind of exegetical study suggested earlier in this book, the Bible's meaning is deepened. It is more than asking the question, What does the Bible say to us, in our time? It is a personal question, asked meditatively in the presence of God. The question now becomes, What is God saying to me in this passage? What leading am I to find for my life today? How does this verse throw light on some area of my life? On some problem with which I have been wrestling?

One's relationship to God becomes an essential part of this approach to the Bible, and it deepens. One begins to acquire an ability to sense nuances in the text that might not have been perceived earlier. Such a reading of John's Gospel, for example, might lead the reader to focus on the "I am" passages and to realize anew the multiple meanings of the metaphors Jesus used concerning himself. Reading one of the letters of Paul in this thoughtful way makes it possible to learn from this man and to grasp his passion for the proclamation of the gospel. We are one with him in hearing God speak. God speaks through the words of the prophets.

Those who approach the Bible directly for spiritual growth may find that one key verse in a particular passage seems to speak directly to them. This can happen with startling clarity. Gospel pericopes frequently conclude with such a verse, but there may be one within the story. The transfiguration passage has several such verses (Luke 9:28-36): the example of Jesus going with the disciples to pray; Peter's suggestion that they remain on the mountain, "not knowing what he said" (misapprehensions are always likely when people speak with God); the voice from the cloud, "This is my Son. Listen to him"; the conclusion, "They kept silent." So many moods and responses!

Learning ever-deeper meanings in Scripture is an enriching experience for the whole of life. The Bible has persisted in having meaning for people thousands of years after it was written because it does more than record the experiences of earlier people who knew God: It is a word through which God continues to speak to people.

No part of the Bible has been more used as a spiritual guide than the book of Psalms. It expresses all the moods any worshiper will have. People who have long sought enrichment for their spiritual lives know it well and can turn to individual psalms as needed. In addition, many have found it helpful to follow the Psalms in sequence, much as monastic communities do. Some follow these in the lectionary, either using the Sunday psalm throughout a week or following the daily lectionary.

Do not stop with the verses you find helpful. Dare to read the passages that are angry and bitter as well as those that express discouragement. Take heart from the psalmist's honesty before God. Try to understand the depths of emotion in these ancient writings and to empathize with the expression of raw human feelings. This will give you insight into ways of praying and into the ways of God.

This education about the meaning of the Psalms is different from the one you get when you study the book's component parts, its structure, or the background of particular psalms. You are at the heart of why the Psalms were written in the first place and why they have been preserved for our spiritual enrichment. The book of Psalms is not only the hymnal of synagogue and church but also the foremost devotional guide for believers.

In his discerning book on prayer, Abraham Joshua Heschel writes:

> The power of the Bible is in its not being absolutely dependent on man's symbolic interpretations. The prophets do not live by the grace of preachers, their words are significant even when taken literally. They do not speak in oracles but in terms of specific actions. *Love thy neighbor as thyself* has a strictly literal meaning, and so has the commandment to observe the Seventh

day. The Bible has tried to teach that holiness is vital, that the things of the spirit are real. The Torah is not in heaven. The voice of God is unambiguous; it is the confusion of man, of the best of us, that creates the ambiguity. It tells us precisely how God wants us to act. Performing a sacred deed we are not aware of symbolizing religion; a sacred act *is* religion.[5]

THE BIBLE IN A SPIRITUAL LIFE GROUP

Biblical material is frequently used in small group study for the enrichment of the spiritual life of members. This differs from individual study in that people are willing to share their deepest insights, to become vulnerable as they attest to their religious experience, and to learn from the insights of others. Such a group meets at a time and place where it will be free from interruptions and distractions. As a small group it will nonetheless avoid limiting itself in such a way as to appear to be an elite group. As members leave and new people join, there is a refreshing change in viewpoints. When the group grows too large, it divides into new groups.

The easiest plan is simply to choose a brief book from the Bible, part of a long writing, or a selection of psalms. This necessitates breaking up the content so that thought can be concentrated on smaller units. As the weeks go by, participants will be able to refer back to earlier sections to deepen their understanding of the passage currently being considered.

In a group setting you might wish to begin with a brief introduction to the book itself: the context of the writing and some observations on critical exegesis. After this background, the focus changes. The question to be asked is, What might God be saying to me in this writing? This is no different from the question asked in a solitary setting, but to speak one's reflections aloud is to hear them in a new way, and particularly to hear them in relation to the responses of others. This is good because it is a check on one's inner thoughts. People are helped by this interchange—both the one who dares to speak and those who listen. Some are likely to find it difficult to speak candidly, and this has to be accepted by everyone. Openness comes gradually as trust builds.

A group might decide to build their reflections around a theme: forgiveness, covenant, redemption, prayer, or some other option. This

5. *Quest for God: Studies in Prayer and Symbolism* (New York: Crossroad, 1982), p. 133.

necessitates careful preparation. Technical books on these subjects will not be helpful, but devotional literature may give some clues. The bimonthly journal *Weavings,* for instance, devotes every issue to one particular theme in the Christian spiritual life, and many articles include appropriate biblical passages.[6]

The format for biblical study in a spiritual life group begins with attention to the passage. Usually one person reads it aloud, then each rereads it silently and slowly. This merges into a period for quiet thought about the passage. Another person then gives a second reading of the passage. In this rhythm, participants listen to a vocal interpretation, then turn inward to hear the passage speak personally, and again turn to listen to a reading aloud, becoming aware of the presence of the group.

The time then comes for sharing reflections. The emphasis is on learning from the insights of others. People build on what they hear said. The Holy Spirit speaks through such a group. Participants discover how the spiritual life of one can enrich that of all. The Bible is the catalyst for such action. In the free interchange that results from meditation and reflection, individuals can receive personal illumination and mutual support.

The time allotted to each phase will depend on the group. A beginning group, still uncertain of the approach, will be less comfortable with a long period of silence than an established group will be. Being together for a number of sessions builds a sense of trust. Some have never considered silence as a way of studying the Bible. A sense of being in the presence of God while reflecting on a particular passage may be new. Others with more experience offer the quiet balance that clues newcomers in to feeling comfortable. Sometimes the passage itself may not seem to offer an opening to deep insights. Here, however, the group process is an advantage. Somebody will find an inspiring word.[7]

A spiritual life group may be formed by open invitation. This will ensure variety by including people who are practiced and those who want to learn this approach. When the initial group has been together long enough to feel comfortable in their sharing, the group may be enlarged by invitation as members think of friends who would find

---

6. *Weavings: A Journal of the Christian Spiritual Life* (Nashville: The Upper Room).
7. This is a form of studying the Bible, classically referred to as *lectio divina* (divine reading). A helpful book is *Bible Reading for Spiritual Growth* by Norvena Vest, Harper San Francisco, 1993. The use of this form for personal meditation is outlined by Thelma Hall in *Too Deep for Words. Rediscovering Lectio Divina,* New York/Mahwah: Paulist Press, 1988.

it helpful. You want to avoid becoming a group that thinks of itself as having a higher level of spirituality than other groups in the parish have. Yours is simply one approach to discerning God's purposes and growing personally in the understanding of the Bible. It is one way of learning.

Some particular points need to be remembered. This kind of group will not emphasize exegesis. Although it may be called into the process to give a needed clue to the setting of a passage or to clarify meaning by reference to the kind of writing it represents, exegesis cannot be a major thrust. Bible study groups offer this kind of learning (see chapter 7). The purpose is not intellectual (critical) understanding but spiritual discernment. These are not mutually exclusive; it is simply a matter of emphasis within the particular purpose of a group.

It is also important to remember that the reflective or meditative portion is essential if the sharing portion is to have any depth. The time spent on silent reflection needs to be lengthened from its initial brief period. Only the person leading the group can know what time span is comfortable and fruitful. God is present, and this is perceived in the working of the group. The depth of the sharing among participants is a direct outgrowth of the spiritual thoughtfulness of individual meditation.

The spiritual life group has a specific task and a clear goal. Participants are helped through shared conversation and through the impetus given toward deepening their personal daily reflection on the Bible. They become part of a mutual support group where people come to know one another's perplexities and assurances as they reflect together on Scripture. As a group they are asking how the Bible gives direction for life and how God's purposes can be perceived through human blindness. The one who made the blind to see and the deaf to hear continues to bring light and life.

Consideration of spiritual development has frequently revolved around what one person does while reading the Bible alone. Serious thought about the procedures, values, and limitations of group Bible study with an emphasis on spiritual growth is important. The group is a form of *koinonia*—a gathering within the believing community for mutual support in their pilgrimage. It is a way of reaching out to people with special needs, and that personal concern is itself an expression of community. Groups like these give newcomers who are invited to join a sense of participating in the life of the parish. The personal welcome into a small group can help them feel at home.

A small group is essential for the many people who hesitate to speak or even to ask a question in a large group. Most people have such a limitation. Everyone feels needed in a small group. Everyone can be heard. Each knows the importance of listening and responding so that personal hesitancy is replaced by a sense of responsibility. With this kind of hearing, it is possible to build on one another's statements.

Small groups are susceptible to becoming ingrown or developing a sense of spiritual superiority, as noted earlier. Intimacy and spiritual growth are a small group's assets; but they can become liabilities. Newcomers will then feel unwelcome. Regular participants will become so accustomed to one another's viewpoints as to be unable to help in sharpening discernment.

For these reasons it may be well to form a group on a limited time basis, a convenanting group where each member promises to attend sessions regularly for a period of time—Advent or Lent, for example, three months, six months, or even a year. Dividing can be a healthful avenue for growth. No parish is likely to have too many spiritual life groups or an oversupply of Bible study groups.

Growing familiarity with the Bible is essential to spiritual growth, both for individuals and for the life of a parish. All members need to learn how God can speak to an individual through meditative reading of the biblical Word. Many will be further enriched as they lend these insights to the reflective study of the Bible in small groups.

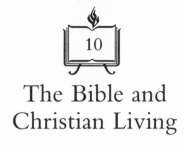

The Bible and Christian Living

CHRISTIANS HAVE ALWAYS LOOKED TO THE BIBLE as the rule for life. They have found in its words security in the midst of the uncertainties of any society. Parents today want their children to "learn the Bible" and expect that the church will provide this. They want this because *they* do not know the Bible, they say, despite the fact that a generation earlier *their* parents sent them to church with precisely the same objective. "Knowing the Bible" or its contents is the means to a desired end: to live a moral life, to grow into good, law-abiding people.

The Bible is spoken of as the Word of God, and this means much more than words about God. The Scriptures tell believers who God is and how God acts. In its pages are written the human response to God. The Bible is therefore a dialogue between God and human beings, creatures of God. For this reason it is essential that Christians know the whole story of the Bible. To choose from it only those sections that seem to give directions for living distorts the full message. Each story, each teaching, is found within a total context of biblical experience.

WHAT IS OBEDIENCE?

There is a security in rules. People know exactly what is expected of them. When they are told that the Bible contains rules that will show them how to live obediently to God, they feel content, even though they realize the seriousness of trying to keep these rules. The secular equivalent is the person who tries to live up to ideals: of honesty, friendship, peace—ideals that can become abstractions.

Keeping rules brings a sense of satisfaction and of accomplishment. Failing to keep rules can be a spur to further effort. It is possible to be a very good person and not to believe in God. Belief in the human capacity to improve and to change society for the better is an enterprise that has brought a challenging life to many.

But the Christian lives by the grace of God. Love is never earned; it is freely given to be freely received. We are loved because we are created by God. Think about how attached people become to a garden they have tended, pottery they have made, a story they have written. Being loved by God cannot be dependent on how carefully the biblical commandments are kept, or even on how hard people try to keep them. The perspective must be turned around. Those who know God's love respond by loving God. Keeping the commandments is a way of showing love toward God.

The result may be the same; the attitude is different. The one who obeys God in order to be approved by God, to be rewarded, or to avoid punishment will live under anxiety. Much of the keeping of laws within a society is based on control by sanctions. To be sure, the majority of citizens are law-abiding because it brings order to life. And those who break the law do so regardless of restraints. Family discipline is frequently based on a reward-punishment basis. Psalm 119 is a glorious hymn of praise to God for Torah, the Teaching. "I treasure your word in my heart, so that I may not sin against you" (v. 11); "I find delight in your commandments, because I love them. I revere your commandments, which I love, and I will meditate on your statutes" (vv. 47-48). Here is a person for whom Torah is a gracious gift of God, and keeping it is a privilege.

Gospel is a proclamation of good news. But if the Christian life were to consist of keeping rules in order to earn God's approval or to receive eternal life, then it would be more of a burden. This is made dramatically apparent in the Sermon on the Mount. Jesus' command to love the enemy is difficult, even when we psychologize it by saying that hatred does harm to the person who hates. The words about not resisting the evildoer are equally difficult to accept.

Remember that these words were addressed to disciples. "When Jesus saw the crowds, he went up to the mountain; and after he sat down, his disciples came to him. Then he began to speak, and taught them" (5:1). He was speaking to people who had accepted his invitation to follow him into an uncertain future. To a scribe who expressed a desire to follow him, Jesus said, "Foxes have holes, and birds of the air have nests; but the Son of Man has nowhere to lay his head" (Matt. 8:20). The disciple leaves the security of boundaries to become wholly dependent on the grace of God. This is what trust means. "Perfect love casts out fear" is the word from 1 John 3:18. What Jesus tried to demonstrate in his life and death is that one who loves God trusts God utterly.

This description of the Christian life as a response to faith is difficult to teach. It does not even fit with the analogy of human family relationships. We know all about accepting each other as we are, but too often love is withheld in displeasure or is expected as a reward. The gospel seems difficult to translate into grace between parent and child. We recognize that we are human, unequal to loving the way God loves. That realization of inadequacy can cause precisely the response the gospel invites: a willing turning toward God for help.

One educator who works with local parishes found that the curriculum materials most sought after were those that would teach moral values based on a biblical pattern. This approach to Christian education is concrete—something to be illustrated and memorized from specific biblical stories and teaching along with illustrations from life experience. It is more difficult to describe the subtle implications of behavior. In his now-classic book *The Vision of God,* Kenneth E. Kirk, Oxford theologian, sets out the doctrine of the *summum bonum*—the highest good for the Christian. In a chapter on "Law and Promise" he describes an approach to life that highly values keeping rules: "A system of thought which is primarily moralistic, insofar as it sets before men a rule of conduct by which it is their first duty to measure themselves, is in essence egocentric. It is only one of the many forms which selfishness can take, even though its rule appears superficially altruistic."[1] He continues by affirming that only when service is performed as part of worship can this be escaped. "Without the spirit of worship, no service can be worthy the name. Disinterested service is the only service that is serviceable; and disinterestedness comes by the life of worship alone."[2]

Following Jesus does not mean trying to do exactly what he did. God calls people to personal forms of commitment. The stories that teach Christian living will be those that describe God's love and the response of the recipient. In the parable of the Pharisee and the tax collector, the despised man—who knew that he was unable to keep the law and only prayed for mercy—was justified in the sight of God

---

1. (London: Longmans, Green & Co., 1931), p. 449.
2. Ibid., p. 541.

(Luke 18:9-14). Self-sufficiency was not enough. This parable confounds all our efforts to teach that if people try hard enough, they will win God's approval.

Recall Luke's narrative about the woman who had sought medical help for twelve years with no cure and then, unseen, approached Jesus in a crowd. His reply was, "Daughter, your faith has made you well; go in peace" (8:43-48). All previous efforts had been in vain; she reached out in faith and God responded.

When people act in response to God, it is possible to accept the reality that doing good is not always rewarded. Jesus taught his disciples that they would be rejected, not received in homes, and abused. We see this every day, read about it, see it on television.

How then are we to teach those fundamental biblical passages: the Ten Commandments, the Beatitudes, the summary of the law? Each has a context. The Ten Commandments were given when the covenant was made between God and Israel on Mount Sinai. The key word is *faithfulness*. God is faithful in covenanting to lead a people. The response of the people is to live in such a way that their actions proclaim them to be God's people. They are different from those in neighboring countries, particularly because they worship God alone and make no idols. They do not earn God's favor; they respond to it. Theologian Hans Küng points out that "the *distinguishing feature* even *of the Old Testament ethos* did not consist in the individual precepts or prohibitions, but in the *Yahweh faith* which meant that all the individual precepts and prohibitions were subordinated to the will of the God of the Covenant."[3] He adds: "*Moral behavior acquires a new motivation:* gratitude, love, the prospect of long life, the gift of freedom become decisive motives."[4]

Jesus referred to acting on his words as being like a wise person who built a house on rock (Matt. 7:24-27). Jesus summarized the law in commandments of God that went far beyond rules: to love God and love the neighbor (Matt. 22:34-40; Mark 12:28-34). On this Küng comments, "The *distinguishing feature* in particular of the *Christian ethos* does not consist in the individual precepts or prohibitions, but in *faith in Christ* for which all the individual precepts or prohibitions are subordinate to Jesus Christ and his rule."[5]

So we will teach these and repeat them to people throughout our lives. No one has ever fully learned them or understood all the implications. But they can be illustrated in the lives of people for whom

---

3. *On Being a Christian,* p. 542.
4. Ibid., p. 543.
5. Ibid., p. 543.

indeed loving God resulted in loving acts on behalf of the neighbor, whoever that might be. We will teach them as gifts of God through which is offered God's presence and power to live the good news.

THE BIBLE AND PERSONAL LIVING

The Bible has been called a pathway and the Christian life described as a pilgrimage. The teaching passages become guideposts. They provide a sense of direction and the assurance of boundaries. In the words of the psalmist, "Your word is a lamp to my feet and a light to my path" (119:105). People prefer that a path be clear, although this does not always happen. They want the brush cut away, the high grass trodden down, all the signposts clearly written and placed where they will be easily seen. So when they look to the Bible as a path giving directions for life, they cannot resist the desire to simplify the teaching in order to make its meaning easy to discern. They would also like to absolutize it, setting aside its ambiguities like brush along the way.

Living in the Christian way is not that easy. The result is that sincere people, devoutly trying to be followers in the way, disagree as to the interpretation of the teaching. They accuse one another of infidelity. They begin to question their own interpretation. They ask themselves whether it is all right to see a biblical passage differently at different times of their lives. The good news is that this ability to discern more in the Bible across the years indicates the living quality of the Word of God. This suggests not a relative aspect to the teaching but, on the contrary, the possibility of diversity in interpretation.

Those who try to observe the teaching perfectly may discover several difficulties. They may assure themselves that they are succeeding, in which case they are surely bending the teaching to their perception, because other people might be interpreting the teaching otherwise. Or they will feel guilty because of their inability to be perfect, in which case they have forgotten that they are not God, and they will break under their impossible task. Those who try hard to suppress anger find that it will not work indefinitely. They need to locate the cause of anger and channel it in ways that do not hurt people. The apostle Paul describes everyone's experience: "I would not have known what it is to covet if the law had not said, 'You shall not covet.' But sin, seizing an opportunity in the commandment, produced in me all kinds of covetousness" (Rom. 7:7b-8a). He goes on to say that the law is holy, the command is just and good, but sin intervenes.

Only God, through the life-giving Spirit in Jesus Christ, overcomes sin and brings life.

So any teaching about Christian living comes up against Paul's affirmation, "All have sinned and fall short of the glory of God; they are now justified by his grace as a gift, through the redemption that is in Christ Jesus" (Rom. 3:23-24). Inevitably the teacher must deal with sin and forgiveness, for this is the only way that obedience can be made bearable.

Notice that in the Gospels Jesus seldom speaks about sin; when he does, he usually includes forgiveness. To those about to stone a woman taken in adultery, he said, "Let anyone among you who is without sin be the first to throw a stone at her" (John 8:7). Asked whether the cause of a man's blindness was his own sin or his parents', Jesus said, "Neither" (John 9:3). "Everyone who commits sin is a slave to sin. . . . So if the Son makes you free, you will be free indeed" (John 8:34, 36). Recognizing the deliberate distortion in accusations leveled against him by those who said that he healed through the rule of demons, Jesus replied, "Whoever speaks against the Holy Spirit will not be forgiven, either in this age or in the age to come" (Matt. 12:32). Jesus shows us who God is and how God acts. In these Gospel passages, Christians are affirmed as they try to live in obedience through lives that witness in compassionate action. They also learn that they will indeed fall short but that, recognizing this, they can receive forgiveness from God who loves them, and power to persevere.

Teaching the Bible as a lifestyle recognizes the limitations of being human. Such teaching will always include what Jesus had to say about sin and forgiveness and will use Paul's experience. The people of the Bible are models and mentors, for they walked with God in their sinfulness as well as in their obedience. Jacob cheated his brother, yet in the Bible he is seen as the progenitor of the tribes of Israel. Moses killed an Egyptian slave driver yet later was called by God to lead his people out of slavery. Saul, David, and Solomon were flawed men, but celebrated as rulers anointed by God. Peter is our example as followers of Jesus: confessing him one day, denying him another; rejoicing in the conversion of a Gentile, and later at Jerusalem hesitating to affirm what he had done.

Some teaching materials give only one answer. When teaching a commandment, such as the one Paul uses, "You shall not covet," they may illustrate with an example that shows a person feeling guilty. This is an easy way to teach because a teacher can reinforce a biblical word with one example but does not have to invite the class to share their questions. People live in a real world, and coveting can bring pleasure!

At what point does coveting become a danger for the Christian life for child, adolescent, or adult? What forms does the struggle take? Good teaching recognizes the need to respond to such questions.

Other materials set out the complexity of the issue and suggest several modes of action. To some teachers, this seems to dilute the biblical message. The Word of the Lord should be clear. Unfortunately it does not appear to be so for everyone. In order to recognize that the Christian life can indeed be a struggle, the more complicated mode of teaching is necessary. God gives people choices, and only in recognizing their own limitations in making these choices will they be likely to turn to God for help.

This balance can help teachers develop another quality they need—that of helping people to become flexible without at the same time feeling that their foundations have been shaken. Those who are rigid in trying to do right need to be assured that their goal is good: Christians have always been recognized by their deeds. With this fundamental established, people can be assured that this goal is not violated when they recognize in themselves or others an inability to live this way fully. They are given good news when they are assured that they live by grace alone.

Another question that arises is whether some biblical teaching is so clearly directed to its original situation that it does not fit today's context or needs modification in order to be applied by Christians today. A teacher needs the inner freedom to permit diversity of interpretation in the expression of opinions and feelings. To discourage this only forces people to withdraw, disagreeing but being unable to discuss the situation. They may be troubled by a perceived conflict between their understanding of a Christian lifestyle and what they are being told it ought to be. Are some sayings commands for everyone and others addressed to those with a particular call? The experience of those in the New Testament church can be helpful. Few teachers would say that there is only one answer to a question.

The Christian lifestyle has been predicated on love, following the two basic commandments. This takes precedence over specific teachings and is assumed to be the motivation for action. God is love, and any understanding of love among humans must arise from this. Dietrich Bonhoeffer writes in his last and incomplete book:

> The biblical concept of love, and it alone, is the foundation, the truth and the reality of love, in the sense that any natural thought about love contains truth and reality only insofar as it participates in this its origin, that is to say, in the love which is God Himself

in Jesus Christ. . . . Love is the reconciliation of man with God in Jesus Christ. The disunion of men with God, with other men, with the world and with themselves, is at an end. Man's origin is given back to him.

Love, therefore, is the name for what God does to man in overcoming the disunion in which man lives.[6]

This affirmation prevents love from sinking into sentimentality. God's love is a suffering and forbearing love, a seemingly severe love that includes judgment while promising that judgment can be fulfilling. For the Christian, human love will likewise encompass joy and pain even unto death. The collect in the Book of Common Prayer for Monday in Holy Week is a powerful affirmation of this love; it begins, "Almighty God, whose most dear Son went not up to joy but first he suffered pain, and entered not into glory before he was crucified . . ."[7] This is the strangeness of the gospel.

Simplicity is another hallmark of the Christian lifestyle. Jesus practiced it with the disciples. We know that God cares for the birds of the air and the flowers of the field. We know that worry will not add a single hour to the span of life. Few of his followers are able to accept his assurance "Do not worry about your life." Jesus asks his people for a singlehearted devotion to the reign of God and to God's righteousness (Matt. 6:25-34).

Some Christians live in communities that practice a simple lifestyle. Others see it in personal terms or as a family decision. Simplicity is a matter of not only having but also doing. The distracted person, rushing to fulfill an overloaded agenda, is far from leading the simple life. A unifying simplicity comes through meditation on Scriptures that help to lift the day's agenda into the presence of God.[8]

Simplicity of life and stewardship are intertwined. Those who live in obedience to God know that all they are and have is a gift of God, and they lovingly return all to God. This is epitomized in the well-known hymn that begins, "Take my life and let it be consecrated, Lord, to thee." It continues, "Take my moments, days, hands, heart, voice, intellect, will, myself." The parable of the talents and verses about giving are involved by those teaching about stewardship. Another biblical example used is the Israelites' donation of jewels for the

---

6. *Ethics* (New York: Macmillan Co., 1955), p. 52.
7. Book of Common Prayer, p. 220.
8. A helpful symposium on this subject is Ronald J. Sider, ed., *Lifestyle in the Eighties: An Evangelical Commitment to Simple Lifestyle* (Philadelphia: Westminster Press, 1982).

building of the tabernacle (Exod. 35:22). The Deuteronomic tithe is quoted yearly for church canvasses. The deeper levels of personal stewardship are understood in the total self-giving of Jesus and in his admonition not to be concerned about one's life. Stewardship of the earth is an outgrowth of this sense of discipleship and of a relationship to God, who created and has redeemed the whole world.

Short-term courses are available on topics related to personal ethical living, with study guides and resource suggestions to help the teacher. A study that uses a series of biblical passages, including those suggested here, will help people as they share insights. Including background from exegetical and theological material will deepen the discussion. Case studies, including human interest stories that appear in the daily newspaper, can be a starting point, as can videotaped television interviews. Role-playing of ethical situations makes vivid an otherwise theoretical situation.

THE BIBLE AND COMMUNITY LIVING

Christians sometimes disagree as to whether the biblical concern is with personal salvation alone or whether social responsibility is included. The previous section discussed how the individual lives as a Christian in personal relationships, following the teaching and seeking to keep the commandments of God in everyday life. But Christians live in a wide world, and individual initiative may not be enough.

The prophets were concerned with social justice. God had made a covenant with Israel, and to worship God truly meant dealing justly with each other. Personal concern was one facet. In the first chapter of Isaiah, this prophet, counselor to kings, announces that God wants no more of their festivals and sacrifices: "I cannot endure solemn assemblies with iniquity. . . . Even when you make many prayers I will not listen; your hands are full of blood" (vv. 13, 15). How then can they be restored to God's favor? "Cease to do evil, learn to do good; seek justice, rescue the oppressed, defend the orphan, plead for the widow" (vv. 16b, 17). There is promise, and warning: "If you are willing and obedient, you shall eat the good of the land; but if you refuse and rebel, you shall be devoured by the sword; for the mouth of the Lord has spoken" (vv. 19-20). They are unjust because they are idolatrous; they have forgotten their God.

Ancient people did not have a notion of individualism as we have today. Each person was an integral part of a family and a state. The king represented this wholeness. Justice was therefore a community matter. Psalm 72, a prayer for the king, begins "Give the king your justice, O God, and your righteousness to a king's son. May he judge your people with righteousness, and your poor with justice. . . . May he defend the cause of the poor of the people, give deliverance to the needy, and crush the oppressor" (vv. 1, 2, 4). Such examples could be multiplied among the writings of the psalmists and the prophets.

Jesus showed compassion toward people of every need. Identifying himself to John the Baptist's disciples, he points out that "the blind receive their sight, the lame walk, the lepers are cleansed, the deaf hear, the dead are raised, and the poor have good news brought to them" (Matt. 11:5). He commended the widow who put two small copper coins in the treasury (Mark 12:43). He announced, "Blessed are you who are poor, for yours is the kingdom of heaven" (Luke 6:20). Paul took offerings for the poor and counseled concern for them in his congregations. He wrote to the congregation at Corinth urging them to give generously to the churches of Macedonia, citing as example "the generous act of our Lord Jesus Christ, that though he was rich, yet for your sakes he became poor, so that by his poverty you might become rich" (1 Cor. 8-9).

This is the personal outreach of Christians. Paul's congregations had no political power, but Christians were recognized in the early centuries because of their concern for the needs of one another and of the outsider. The prophets spoke to an independent land when social obligations for justice devolved upon the whole people and their rulers. There is no split between individual and societal responsibility for those who live the gospel.

Christians have long been concerned about their responsibility in time of war and civil unrest. Stories from the early centuries of the church tell of those who refused to serve in the Roman army and were martyred. When the church itself became involved with political power, the attitude changed. The doctrine of "just war" was enunciated. The Reformation saw the rise of distinctly pacifist communities, which continue today, including the Mennonites, the Church of the Brethren, and, founded in the seventeenth century, the Society of Friends. This is a social issue that persists. The prophets' vision of turning swords into plowshares and spears into pruning hooks (Isa. 2:4 and Mic. 4:3) is reversed in Joel 3:10. What does this mean? Is a world without war an eschatological vision? In Matt. 26:52, as Jesus was being arrested, he said to Peter, "All who take the sword will perish by the sword." Then what is to be made of Jesus' admonition to his disciples in Luke 22:36 just before they went to the garden: "now the one who has no sword must sell his cloak and buy one," and being assured that they had two swords, he replied, "It is enough." These two passages are juxtaposed here in order to demonstrate that readers can prooftext to affirm their own conclusions. Without a study of the written context, the setting for the writing, and the intention of the writer, more than one interpretation is possible. The ministry of Jesus—his life, death, and resurrection—are the answer, but not a simple one. Thousands have died sacrificially in wars. Others have died in nonviolent resistance. The question, What would Jesus do? does not supply an answer, for the outcome of living as a Christian is ambiguous. Christians are commanded to love one another as Jesus loved them and laid down his life for them. Loving through life-threatening differences is painful, and to some impossible.

Many people explore social concerns by using the action-reflection model. In this approach, people are involved in a situation, after having been prepared for the experience, and later reflect together on what happened. They analyze it not only in sociopolitical and economic terms, but in the light of biblical narrative and teaching and in consideration of how one might act as a Christian. This method becomes Christian education only when both the situation and the immediate experience are considered seriously under the cross and resurrection.[9]

The interaction of individual and community responsibility is nowhere more clearly seen than in the current concern for the environment. On the one hand is personal lifestyle, which for Christians means simplicity of life, however interpreted; on the other hand is the necessity for community guidelines, including the involvement of business, government, and church. This concern is most frequently addressed out of the fear that by abusing the environment—including other creatures—we are destroying ourselves. Both the statement of concerns and the solutions are based on the assumption that we are the center of life on earth and that creation should serve our needs. To act beneficently is self-service. This way of thinking is challenged by James M. Gustafson, who, in his thought-provoking writings, has probed the Christian dimension of ethics. He affirms that in a theocentric view of the universe, God is the center. Therefore human beings must see themselves in an interacting relationship to every part of creation.[10] As long as humans work to restore the environment to

---

9. Two books with methods for teaching social justice are Suzanne C. Toton, *World Hunger: The Responsibility of Christian Education* (Maryknoll, N.Y.: Orbis Books, 1982); and James McGinnis et al., *Educating for Peace and Justice: Religious Dimensions* (St. Louis: Institute for Peace and Justice), 1985.

10. *Theology and Ethics* (Chicago: University of Chicago Press, 1981); and *Ethics from a Theocentric Perspective,* vol. 2, *Ethics and Theology* (Chicago: University of Chicago Press, 1984).

wholeness because they believe their species is central, they will not accomplish their goal. Christians must see the need to place themselves in a harmonious partnership with all of God's earth.

THE ETHIC OF JESUS AND CHRISTIAN LIVING

The cross is at the center of life for the Christian. The cross is the consummation of Jesus' life (John 19:30). Through it he fulfilled God's purpose in ways that are still strange even to his followers, because his death seemed to put an end to everything for which he had lived. True, the resurrection is the vindication, but first one must deal with the cross. This is not what modern life is all about. Success is supposed to bring all sorts of good results, apparent for everyone to see.

Dietrich Bonhoeffer, who himself suffered this kind of "success," describes the mystery of the cross through which people are somehow reconciled to God. "In a world where success is the measure and justification of all things the figure of Him who was sentenced and crucified remains a stranger and is at best the object of pity. The world will allow itself to be subdued only by success. It is not ideas or opinions which decide, but deeds. Success alone justifies wrongs done."[11] He continues:

> The figure of the Crucified invalidates all thought which takes success for its standard. Such thought is a denial of eternal justice. Neither the triumph of the successful nor the bitter hatred which the successful arouse in the hearts of the unsuccessful can ultimately overcome the world. . . . It was precisely the cross of Christ, the failure of Christ in the world, which led to His success in history, but this is a mystery of the divine cosmic order and cannot be regarded as a general rule even though it is repeated from time to time in the sufferings of His Church. Only in the cross of Christ, that is, as those upon whom the sentence has been executed, do men achieve their true form.[12]

This speaks disquietingly to Christians in their everyday life. It poses painful decisions. Every day's newspaper and every evening's televised news, testify to the power of personal decisions radically to alter the life of a nation. These challenge the optimists who have given

11. *Ethics,* p. 75.
12. Ibid., p. 77, 78.

assurance that there are easy paths to responsible living. We are faced with the necessity of proclaiming anew a gospel that insists the cross must precede the resurrection. Without death there is no complete life. In a culture that would like to name itself Christian, this is an uncomfortable truth that even Christian teachers within the community of the church find painful. We would like to confine the cross to Holy Week, with its beautiful, moving services, climaxed by all the dazzling beauty of a flower-bedecked cancel for Easter. To be faithful, those who teach must confront a class or a congregation with the meaning of the cross for each individual, for the church, the community, and the world.

The parables do not bring any comfort. Consider Christ's judgment on the nations. The Son of man called into his presence those who had given food and clothing to those in need, who had welcomed the stranger, and had visited those in prison (Matt. 25:31–46). These are not easy tasks, as those who are engaged in these acts of compassion today know.

Teaching the gospel as Christian living will never be easy. It requires two ways of reading the Bible. One way looks at its composition, the context out of which a passage came, its sociological, political, and historical situation. These help learners to grasp both the background and the meaning of a passage for those to whom it was addressed. A second way of interpreting the Word of God requires reading a brief passage deeply in the presence of God, alert to what God might be saying within even a sentence, a phrase, or a word. This balance is what gives fullness to Christian teaching.

Out of this approach, learners can ask the meaning of a passage for them in their daily life and that of their church, community, or nation. Inevitably there will be distortion. Human beings have a need for self-justification. We imagine ourselves to be what we desire to be. This is where members of a committed group can gently correct and reinforce one another.

The meaning of the Christian life is discerned by those who write novels, plays, and short stories, even though these are not explicitly Christian. They are concerned with revealing truth, and they involve participants compellingly. When Henrik Ibsen wrote the play *An Enemy of the People,* he was depicting in contemporary terms a prophet's rejection for announcing a coming disaster, pinpointing the cause, and warning the people to change the situation. John Steinbeck's novel *Grapes of Wrath* chronicles the lives of a displaced people as surely as the Old Testament writings do.

We are in a line of succession from those who for almost two thousand years have sought to witness to Jesus through their lives. They had faith that their witness would not be in vain and that God would raise up others in their place. We are those others. We need to know what they have done. We need also to hear those who are witnesses today in our own parishes and communities. The worldwide immediacy of television can bring to the screen the living presence of others whom we might not otherwise see who can reveal the biblical faith to us in action.

The enterprises through which individuals and congregations reach out to witness complete the teaching responsibility. Through many avenues Christian people join their neighbors in the covenant for whom *mitzvoth,* the doing of good deeds, is essential to keeping Torah. It is our path as Christians to fulfill the teachings of our Lord, Jesus Christ, by following in the way of the cross.

The Bible is central to every form of Christian education. The content will be studied in scholarly fashion, and its theological understandings explored. Methods of teaching will be developed with reference to the needs of each age level. The preeminent role of worship in Christian nurture and education will be realized, and the wellsprings of spiritual life will grow from the biblical Word. All of these will contribute to the witness of the Christian life.

In the midst of that quietly foreboding last evening of Jesus' earthly life, he told his disciples that they were no longer servants but friends. "You did not choose me but I chose you. And I appointed you to go and bear fruit, fruit that will last, so that the Father will give you whatever you ask him in my name." He spoke of the advocate, the Spirit of truth. "You are to testify because you have been with me from the beginning" (John 15:15-17, 26-27).

"Take courage," he declared. "I have conquered the world!" (16:33).

INDEXES

AUTHOR INDEX

SUBJECT INDEX